AFTERworld

The Journey of Life after Life

Scott Alexander King

To dear Lisa thankyou for everything ... the foreword, the support and the friendship ♡♡ xxx

appublishing

Animal Dreaming Publishing
www.animaldreamingpublishing.com

AFTERworld

The Journey of Life after Life

AFTERworld
The Journey of Life after Life

ANIMAL DREAMING PUBLISHING
PO Box 5203 East Lismore NSW 2480
AUSTRALIA
Phone +61 2 6622 6147
www.animaldreamingpublishing.com
www.facebook.com/AnimalDreamingPublishing

First published in 2018
Copyright text © Scott Alexander King
www.animaldreaming.com
Copyright butterfly illustrations © Karen Branchflower
Copyright Afterworld map © Beau Ravn

ISBN 978-0-6481820-3-0

This book is intended for spiritual and emotional guidance only. It is not intended to replace medical assistance or treatment.

Designed by Animal Dreaming Publishing
Printed in Australia

For Joy

With thanks to Tyna King who acted as my scribe many moons ago and in doing so, helped to bring this book to fruition.

Contents

List of Illustrations

Foreword

Death certainly makes us think about life.

Everyone copes with death differently and it will undoubt-edly make a huge impact on your life. It's a very personal experience and there is no right or wrong in how you process what has just happened.

Sometimes it's about survival and coping; dealing with life as it changes in ways we never expected. And where we go about our daily activities surviving each moment by focusing only on our breath to keep us centred.

Navigating the waters of change is challenging enough, and it's heightened when you are also thrown into grief, unexpectedly or not. But I believe that understanding death can help you in this testing process. Nothing will take away the pain or hurt, but insight can ease the space of emptiness and void and give you some hope that life continues in the afterlife.

Being present at someone's passing is one of the most beautiful and intimate experiences that you can ever undergo. You are witnessing the ultimate surrender of a soul into a space that many are scared to go to... the unknown. Yet death is going 'home' and is as easy as falling asleep and waking up in another dimension surrounded by friends, family and loved ones who are there to welcome and guide the soul that has crossed over.

It never ceases to amaze me how Spirit connects with us, whether it's through signs in our everyday life, dreams that seem to be real, or the messages of love that come through those with the gift of mediumship. As a medium, it's incredible to be part of such an experience and it's an honour to open that connection and serve Spirit unconditionally. Throughout the many years I have been practising, I've been blessed to have thousands of spirits share with me the process of transition that they often refer to as a 'rebirth'.

Within these pages you will discover the truth and reality of Spirit in its journey of growth interwoven with beautiful and captivating personal experiences – all of which can help us to understand what happens when we die. You will also discover mixed cultural practices for those who are left trying to live a life in the void that death often creates.

Thank you, Scott, for your insight and strength that you bring to the world.

Lisa Williams
Psychic medium

Introduction

Unlike others who have written books about the Afterworld, I am not a practising medium. Sure, I am known for my psychic abilities and my connection to the animal kingdom and the natural world, but I am not a medium. My experience in this area stems solely from my desire to understand something that is essentially impossible to understand and as such, I would expect your understanding to be different from mine.

For me, the Afterworld as a concept is best described as something that's 'known to be unknowable'. Despite this, I've written this book from notes taken during many years of listening to others speak about the subject, my own spiritual journey and personal experiences, and hundreds of hours of research. I believe that my book is unique in the market because I've haven't penned it from a medium's perspective, nor have I filled it with countless case studies, interviews, stories gleaned from clients or accounts of others' near-death experiences. Instead, this is a journal of sorts written from the perspective of guy whose head was once filled with questions and has now found peace in the answers he found, and who simply wants to communicate what he's learned; to walk hand in hand with you sharing his vision of the Afterworld on a personal level, so that it may help you formulate your own answer to the million-dollar question: 'What happens when we die?'

It's also important to note that I don't intend to prove anything as fact, or to claim that I'm an expert on death, dying or the Afterworld. The notions of death and our journey to the Afterworld are both so profoundly abstract that to claim to be an expert on either would, in my opinion, be a blatant lie. Despite what many may argue, no one can be totally sure of what happens after we pass away. That aspect of our humanly existence cannot be documented or proven as fact, by me or anyone. Even if I had died and returned to write this book, it still could only ever be written from my perspective and I still wouldn't be able to state: 'This is fact'.

I believe that everyone has their own spiritual truth, and I am no different. Spiritual truth is designed to be personal and it matters not how we interpret or express it because it's intended to be different for everyone. It cannot be validated or disproved and therefore cannot be described as 'the one truth' or the 'only truth' or an untruth. It just is, and always will be. So long as we live our truth with no expectation or desire to have anyone else adopt it as their own, then we will always be a living example of what spirituality is and was always meant to be: a personal exploration and expression of the bigger picture.

While this book has given me somewhere to put the answers to many of my questions about the Afterworld, I can't help but wonder whether your mind works in much the same way and that your need to find your own truth is as deeply ingrained as mine? I truly hope it brings you at least peace and comfort and that it does its job by raising even more questions, because even after reading it one truth will remain: no one can know for sure what happens when we die.

The gift of Oneness

As a young person I truly believed that life was a case of 'me against the world', that everyone was 'only in it for themselves' and that the only person I could completely trust was me. I had no reason to doubt my beliefs because the prominent people in my life constantly confirmed and anchored my rather limited and tainted view.

And that's how it was until one fateful night in January of 1995 when two good friends, who were like brothers to me, were killed in a terrible car accident. My world literally came crashing down and sent me, my values, beliefs and my life into a veritable vortex of darkness, confusion and despair; a whirlpool that promised to either break or make me. However, as though guided by a force beyond my conscious understanding, I instinctively chose to let it make me, thus unwittingly anchoring the spiritual foundation that had already, without my knowledge, nurtured me since I was born and that continues to sustain me to this day. As strange as it may sound, the night my friends were killed and my 'old life' ended was when I first realised I was not alone. That night part of me died with my friends but in many ways, all of me was reborn. I lost something I will never, ever get back; something that filled my heart with hope and purpose while making my past more superficially bearable.

On losing this sacred 'something', though, I discovered over time that I had gained more than I could ever have hoped for. In receiving the lesson of loss, I simultaneously gained the gift of Oneness. As I mourned my loss, I came to realise that its essence had returned to the Great Mystery. It had returned to Great Spirit, to be reunited with the Source of all Life, the source of my own spirit and life force. What I had lost was quickly returned in a way that inspired connectedness to all people and all things of Nature. Although I could no longer see or touch it in the physical sense, I could feel it everywhere. I suddenly felt an alliance with the world that I had never really believed existed before, let alone ever hoped to experience first-hand. I realised that although I was still alone in the physical sense, on a spiritual level I was surrounded by Great Spirit – a realisation that 'woke me up'. It literally helped me to reclaim my purpose and welcome back my soul's essence.

PART ONE

Mapping the Journey to the AFTERworld

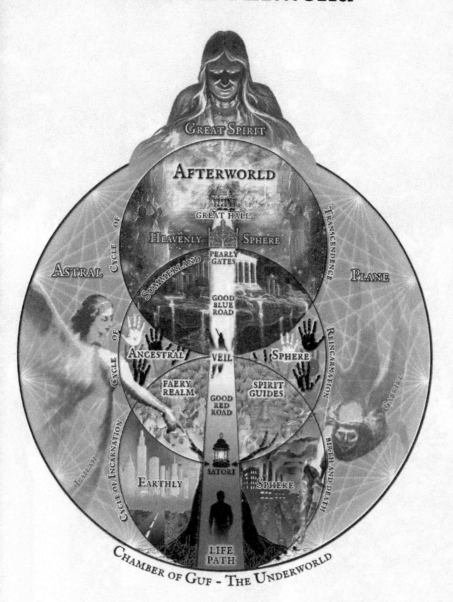

GREAT SPIRIT

AFTERWORLD

GREAT HALL

HEAVENLY SPHERE

ASTRAL

PLANE

PEARLY GATES

SUMMERLAND

GOOD BLUE ROAD

ANCESTRAL

VEIL

SPHERE

FAERY REALM

SPIRIT GUIDES

GOOD RED ROAD

SATORI

EARTHLY

SPHERE

LIFE PATH

CYCLE OF TRANSCENDENCE

CYCLE OF REINCARNATION

CYCLE OF BIRTH AND DEATH

CYCLE OF INCARNATION

LAILAH

GABRIEL

CHAMBER OF GUF - THE UNDERWORLD

Of God and Great Spirit

As a child I believed my feelings of aloofness were only aimed at the external world, but as I healed and grew, I realised I had also been completely detached from myself. The gift hidden within the lesson of loss mentioned above helped me to see that to be embraced by the world, I first had to embrace myself; that how I felt about myself determined how the world responded to me.

If you decide to feel isolated then you will be, especially when you have not welcomed yourself 'home'. If you have an issue with living in your own skin, then how can you expect yourself to feel comfortable living anywhere else? And most importantly, how can you expect others to feel comfortable living with you? So, to welcome myself home, I journeyed back to the earliest negative experience I could consciously remember and forced myself to relive it... in minute detail. I forced myself to feel every emotion, ask every question and to witness every aspect. I was literally there, amid it all... I cried and cried and cried. I felt my heart being ripped out all over. I felt it break and then break again. I screamed at Great Spirit. I yelled and cursed and swore – and I meant every word. I figured that if Great Spirit had put me through all that, then there had to be a reason – a very good reason. Spirit must have known what it was doing. It must have been planned and must have considered me worthy, if you like. I decided that if I could go back to that first experience, that moment as a small child that put me in a box and labelled me as 'damaged', and if I reviewed it for flaws, I then might find the reason for why Great Spirit did that.

I decided I would view that first experience like a pebble and that if I threw it into the emotional pool that was my life, the ripples that fanned out would help me address every other incident that had happened since then, a bit like dominoes. I threw that pebble with all my might and in reliving the experience, I realised that I hadn't consciously done anything to deserve it. I then asked Great Spirit: 'Why would I need to experience that?' I was 'told' that it was part of my spiritual training, my apprenticeship. It was the beginning of a learning from which powerful experiences would be gleaned; experiences that would offer me wisdom in my future, so long as I took the time to learn the lesson hidden in the learning.

And so, I did. I honoured my sacred learning and then realised I had to do the same with every aspect of my life and above all, with my most recent loss. With greater confidence and desperate to heal, I painfully reviewed that too and eventually discovered the lesson within. It was then that I felt Great Spirit and the realisation of the true beauty that Great Spirit represents.

Up until this point I had always believed that God lived 'out there' and that to be close to him was almost impossible. God had always been out of reach, unobtainable and to be feared. But I had misunderstood. I alone had placed him out there, God hadn't. The day I realised this was the day I found Oneness. I had been using the wrong words and looking at what God represented from the wrong perspective. I had believed what I had read and what I had been told and I had listened to people who had been doing the same thing. I then stopped using the word God and I began using words I had always known and trusted, but had never truly felt or understood: Great Spirit. I felt a stronger connection to those words because they symbolised something I'd always known deep within myself. When I said the words Great Spirit, I felt them at my core and they brought tears to my eyes. But when I uttered the word God, the tears that emerged were triggered by different emotions, including betrayal and rejection. So, God became Great Spirit, and with Great Spirit as my ally, I marched out into the world and found myself. I found my place and I found the people, and for the first time I knew I was one of the people, not apart from them.

For me, Great Spirit is our link to Creation, inspired all of Creation and is Creation. When I refer to Great Spirit, I refer to those in spirit. I refer to the life force inherently found in our brothers and sisters, in plants, trees and stones, in animals and birds and in water, fire, wind and earth. I refer to the power of thought, the emotion of love, the power of silence and the process known as death. And I refer to the people. Great Spirit is what binds us together. It is what makes us 'One'.

When the Western mind thinks of God, we tend to picture the image of a man, probably sporting a long white beard, wearing robes of white, gold sitting on a throne-like chair, and surrounded by white light, Angels and the spirits of those who have passed away. Perhaps seated next to him on a smaller throne is his son, Jesus. But this is not how I envision it.

While there are similarities between the story of how God created life with the creation stories of most cultures, I don't see the Creator as a singular deity. Instead, I envision the Creator as an energy that exists in and exudes from all things of Nature. For me, it is an abstract force that embodies both creation and spirituality, innately found flowing through all things that hold or exhibit the presence of life force. For this reason, I acknowledge Great Spirit and offer thanks because, as a child of the Earth Mother, I recognise myself as being part of all things.

The Chamber of Guf

Before we can explore what the journey of the soul through the Afterworld may entail, we need to investigate where the soul purportedly originates and how it all begins. One explanation that I deeply resonate with has roots in Jewish mysticism. Apparently, the human soul (or 'body') is referred to in Hebrew as the Guf (sometimes spelled Guph or Gup), and the Chamber of Guf, also known as the Treasury of Souls, is where all unborn human souls are stored, waiting for their time to incarnate.

Replenishing the Chamber of Guf is a mighty tree called the Tree of Life, or the Tree of Souls, that, instead of generating seeds from its flowers as regular trees do, produces new souls that fall into the Chamber of Guf where they are collected by Archangel Gabriel who entrusts them to Lailah, the Angel of Conception, who then protects them until they are born. Incidentally, because the sparrow is said to be the only living creature capable of watching the soul's descent from the Chamber of Guf, the Chamber is also affectionately known as the Birdhouse, which explains the sparrow's joyful song.

The Good Red Road of Life

I love my wife with all my heart and I cherish all three of my children. I truly feel blessed to have been given the opportunity to have my own loving, supportive family, and that these beautiful souls volunteered to fill a void in my life. What's even more magical is that outside them exists another circle of good, true and loyal souls that are more like an extended family to me than simply friends. And surrounding them is yet another layer of good people that make up our broader community; people we have come to see as mutually meaningful and important because we improve the quality of one another's lives without ever needing to enjoy a coffee together. And of course, surrounding them is another wider circle of souls, and around them, yet another ... and so it goes on until we finally realise that we are all connected and part of the same overlapping, interlinking, everlasting circle known as the Circle of Life.

We are told from a young age to live a good life; to walk the Good Red Road of Life with honour, respect and dignity. (The Good Red Road being the path known as life whereas the Good Blue Road is the path we follow back to the Creator after we die.) We are encouraged to be an honest person, to do our best in all that we do, to strive to be happy, to follow our dreams and to do what we can to always broaden the Circle of Compassion so that it touches as many souls as it can. Life is especially good, we are told, if we make something of ourselves and do what we can to make our lives meaningful. And it's during this early stage that we often start to realise that life is one giant round-about, and not wishing to sound ungrateful, greedy or rude, we therefore don't question it. We simply push on, feeling the sun on our face and the wind in our hair, stopping occasionally to smell the roses like we are told to do. But we resist asking questions such as, 'How?' and 'Why?' because we don't want to let anyone down. Instead, we strive toward the dream of one day owning a house with a picket fence, a border collie and 2.3 children by waking up early every morning, going to work, coming home, having dinner and going back to bed. Day after day after day. In between we may be fortunate enough to spend our weekends mowing the lawns, going to the park, watching football, visiting the beach or going for a lovely drive in the country. And when we have earned our annual leave, we might take a well-deserved holiday for a few weeks, buy heaps of souvenirs and party until the early hours of the morning. Life is good. Really good.

I can't help but notice that most of us live our lives without sparing any real thought to why we do what we do. We never really ask ourselves: 'What is all this for?' 'What's the point in working hard, achieving greatness, finding love and settling down, having kids and starting a family or accumulating wealth and possessions... if at the end of the day we're going to die anyway?' It's a tough nut to crack – realising we aren't going to be around forever. Sure, we can tell ourselves we're doing it for our kids or to make our parents proud, but in truth... what is the truth? What's it really all about? I guess the only answer I can give is the one that affords me some degree of peace, and that is: 'No one knows for sure.' It brings me some peace because it's the truth but, for me, knowing something is the truth often isn't enough and I cannot help but ask further questions because it's only someone else's truth and I need more than that. I need to find my own truth because when the time comes for me to draw my final breath, I need to know that what happens next is familiar. I need to believe that I'll be a little prepared when I arrive.

From the moment we are born, we essentially begin the journey toward our inevitable death. Our very first breath is taken in preparation for when we take our last. The first breath and the last are dear friends. They honour each other's existence and they happen if only to measure our time on Earth. The processes of birth and death are both miracles and, from my observations, not that dissimilar. They're such abstract concepts; rites of passage that we all face in our lifetime, yet are totally beyond the mere mortal mind to grasp or comprehend in their totality. Yet we celebrate them for the memories they make, the tears they inspire, the laughter they ignite and the confusing, mixed emotions they trigger. No one alive hasn't not asked or pondered questions like: 'Where did I come from?' and 'Where will I go when I die?' We fear yet welcome birth and death for the same but opposing reasons; we anticipate them with wonder on one hand and face them with unease on the other. When a baby is born, for example, the bliss we feel as new parents is immediately and perhaps unconsciously overshadowed with an inherent dread that something bad may happen. When someone passes away – ideally from old age – we comfort ourselves by reassuring one another that we're happy that they're 'no longer in pain' or that they're with family and friends but in truth, we secretly resent them for leaving us behind. It's human nature and it's normal.

Birth and death are chapters of life so deeply shrouded in mystery and wonder that they often leave us speechless and confused when we experience them first-hand because they trigger elated feelings of both joy and grief that, when consciously explored, are so innately joined they could almost be mistaken for one and the same. I was present for the birth of my three children, for example, and I've watched as loved ones have taken their final breath, and both experiences were beautiful, magical and deeply personal; experiences I feel blessed to have witnessed and for which I would readily volunteer myself again, if only to sit one more time in the indescribable, mystical in-between space they both expose me to. It's a sacred space that is real yet fleeting; a space that is neither here nor there, sad nor happy, good nor bad, real nor unreal. It just is. It's filled with wonder and frozen in time where nothing matters, where no one can touch us and where we feel the closest we've ever felt to the Creator. During what feels like hours, those few moments of Hallowed Light fill us with such incredible purity and happiness that we could be forgiven for believing we'd found paradise.

Even though my childhood wasn't ideal, and I no longer associate myself with my birth family and many friends I once loved as family have dropped away for one reason or another, when I stop and think about all the things I've seen, experienced and faced growing into the man I am today, I can't help but think: 'I've lived a good life.' When I ponder all the things that have happened to me, the good and the bad, the things that I have made happen and the things that I've made happen for others, knowingly or not, I can't help but feel grateful because without these experiences I wouldn't be who I am. I don't know who I may have become if I had experienced different situations, but no one can ever expect to know such things. All I can do is to feel grateful for the light that has emerged from the darkness of my past, and to use it to illuminate my future.

But this is simply my view of the world and my place in it. It's my expression of gratitude for the life I've lived and I'm still living. I can't speak for you or other people who, hopefully unlike you, may have forgotten how to ask questions, to wonder or to even think for themselves when it comes to bigger picture topics. I'm reaching out to those people in the hope that by offering potential answers to the countless questions that plague my mind about why I'm here, what the greater purpose of my life is and what happens when I die, I may be able to help them ponder the deeper mysteries of their lives, their mortality and to find a sense of peace in the knowing that there is a master plan, that there is a bigger picture, and that their existence on this beautiful blue and green planet holds greater implications.

Grief

I am grief and I will hold your hand and your heart.
I will help you explore the depths of your feelings and raise
you up once again into the light. Acknowledge me and work
with me and you will once again know joy.

– Jude Downes, author of *From Grief to Goddess*

Grief is a tricky thing. It is a deeply personal road that must be travelled alone. It's a journey that cannot be prepared for, planned or pre-determined. No one can be sure how it will feel like until we're in its midst, nor how it will unfold or affect us long term. Grief affects everyone differently because everyone's reason for suffering it is unique to them. Grief can either make or break the person suffering it. Similarly, and just as dramatically, it can affect their relationships, their family dynamics and, depending on the magnitude and reason for the grief, threaten to divide their entire community. Grief can turn good, happy people into bitter, angry souls, or arrogant, self-important folk into humble, grateful, inwardly aware individuals.

All I know is, grief can prove to be our worst enemy or our dearest friend and companion depending on how and why it strikes, how we deal with it, and what we choose to do with its legacy. I've known couples, for example, who once lived their lives joined at the hip by the sheer power of love, drift apart and separate because the grief of losing their child was too emotionally tortuous to bear, with the very sight of one another proving too painful a reminder of their once perfect life. I've known people who without fail opened their hearts and home every Friday night to friends who had nowhere else to be, so that they could relish in the joy and celebrate the blessing of 'family' only to, after losing a significant family member, emotionally shut down, become morose and self-absorbed, and systematically remove friends once considered old and dear from their lives forever. On the other hand, I've seen people who could easily have been crippled by the sheer weight of their grief make a conscious decision not to succumb to the burden dumped on their soul but to, instead, transform it into something productive in the hope that their personal darkness may shed light for others who have endured a similar pain.

From a shamanic perspective, it is believed that when a person experiences trauma (of any sort), including the death of a friend or family member, they don't just retreat into their subconscious mind to better understand what's happened, but rather a part of our soul or soul essence essentially leaves the body or 'steps aside' so that we may move forward and do what needs to be done. We see this often after a death when, leading up to the funeral and then at the wake afterward, family and friends of the deceased may talk about them as if they're still alive, joking and laughing and appearing outwardly unaffected by their passing. It's like they have become numb to the emotional world, devoid of the ability to feel sad, happy or annoyed, and are effectively shutting down so they can simply carry on. The person is alive but no longer 'living' to the truest meaning of the word.

It is normal, however, for the soul essence to return to the body after a time to allow the suffering person to integrate the experience of their loss and to heal. But sometimes, if the pain is extreme, intense or overwhelming, the soul essence may fail to return, rendering the sufferer incomplete, numb and in a constant state of grief. Sometimes a person may have difficulty reconnecting with their life essence and when this happens, it is believed their life essence has become lost, unable to find its way back to the person leaving them feeling depressed, distrustful and unwell within themselves. They may appear anxious, muddled, clumsy or constantly exhausted. They may become obsessed spiritually or unhealthily fixated on the reason for their trauma.

It was once the traditional role of the shaman (an individual gifted with the ability to soul-journey to other realities or non-ordinary dimensions by means of trance or deep meditation) to journey on behalf of the sufferer in a bid to find and retrieve the soul parts or essences deemed lost and to encourage their return 'home' where they would be reunited with the ailing person. This process was, and is still, referred to as 'soul retrieval'.

I was so broken after my friends were killed in the car accident. So much so, I seriously considered taking my own life. After all the abuse and neglect I had suffered through most of my younger years, the grief I felt after the accident was like the straw that broke the camel's back and I worried that I would never get through it. It wasn't so much that they'd died, but that I was being expected to endure even more pain and confusion. Why had they died? Why them?

I remember a few days after the accident, laying half asleep on my friend's couch, looking through bleary eyes at the still-glowing embers in their fireplace to see the number 97 hovering, glowing red, just above the fire-box. I should have been surprised to see it there, but I wasn't. Instead, I remember thinking, 'What does the number 97 mean?' Well, the accident had occurred in 1995 and only two years later I married my wife and conceived our daughter on our honeymoon. Light found in darkness. Hope realised as a direct result of loss. To this day I believe that my friends came to me that night, to show me that if I could just hold on until 1997, my life would change for the better; that I would find meaning for the things I had experienced and everything would be okay. They had offered me a lifeline by dying. And I took it. How could I not? Had I rolled over and ignored the glowing number 97 and indeed ended my life as I had pondered, perhaps their purpose for dying would have been lost, and their tragic passing would have been in vain. While it didn't lessen my grief, my decision to honour their death gave me strength to go on. Put simply, the day my friends died was the day I decided to start living my life. That was the day my soul essence came home, having been lost to me since my childhood but called back by grief.

I remember asking a counsellor why, after someone dies, grief often brings out the worst in people, even close members of the deceased's own family. She explained that there are two different types of grief: 'Pure grief' and 'complicated grief'. Pure grief, she explained, is the grief we experience after losing someone whose relationship we have done everything in our power to heal, improve and find peace with. While we may love members of our family, we don't always like them – meaning, we may inherently love someone, but not like, support or respect the character traits or behaviour they choose to exhibit. But, when we allow love to prevail and we make peace with those perceived faults by taking time to discuss past hurts that may have caused us to feel confusion, anger and other negative emotions, when they eventually pass from this world, all that's left is the sadness we feel for their loss and the emptiness we experience because they're no longer physically in our life. Having taken the time to talk, all the confusion, anger, resentment and other negative emotions we may have previously harboured are allowed to die with them and we are able to grieve the soul we knew them as, instead of judging them for the qualities we perceived them as favouring.

Complicated grief, on the other hand, is the result of handling things in the polar-opposite way. Instead of taking the time to heal a relationship before the person dies, for example, those destined to experience complicated grief will tend to avoid the person during their last days, weeks and even years of life, preferring to hold onto feelings of anger and resentment. Instead of finding it within themselves to even consider the option to forgive or to talk about past hurts and confusions, the person destined to experience complicated grief will opt to nurture blame and even denial, seemingly doing everything in their power to almost punish the person for being selfish in this way. The trouble dealing with approaching loss in this way is that, after the death takes place, grief is often heavily tainted with feelings of regret, guilt and shame, thus complicating the process because they realise they will never again get the chance to put things right, find peace or bid a heartfelt farewell.

The funeral

An important stage of the grieving process, when we finally acknowledge the need to 'let go' and allow ourselves the opportunity to farewell our loved ones before sending them off on the next leg of their journey, is the funeral or, if the physical body is not present, the memorial service. A funeral is an event that may differ from one culture to the next, but that universally centres on the ceremonial disposal of the body after a person has died.

During a funeral, family, friends and other members of the community may gather to bear witness by giving up the dead by means of cremation, burial or internment, remembering and respecting the departed by mourning their death and celebrating their life, helping the deceased reach the Afterworld, and offering support and sympathy to those left behind. Whether the event is a big funeral with many mourners and an open or closed coffin offered in an official setting, or a small, informal memorial service that involves a casual gathering of close friends and immediate family in a private, meaningful place with (perhaps) just the ashes of the deceased, makes little difference. The purpose of the funeral or service is to help us come to terms with life after death, as opposed to life before death, by offering opportunity to acknowledge that someone we love has died, to give us the chance to say goodbye, to make offerings we believe will support the dead as they embark on their journey such as floral tributes and personal items, to provide a sense of con-tinuity and hope for those left behind, to allow us time to reflect on the greater meaning of life and death, and to establish – if required – a support system within our community intended to help us come to terms with our loss.

What lot of us either don't consider or we may ponder but feel guilty putting too much thought into is that the spirit of our loved ones (or rather, the aspect of the United Element that remains on the Astral Plane) are usually involved in the preparations and lead-up to their own funeral and the wake afterwards. They hear all their friends and family members discussing their life and the things they got up to during life. They hear recollections of all the happy times as well as the sad. They see and hear everything, including the discussions regarding wills and the settling of estates. They witness the tears, the grief and the emptiness that come with loss and the part that many of us don't consider is that they also feel what we feel. Just because they're the ones that have died doesn't mean they don't feel cheated, sad or empty at the thought of losing those they've left behind.

Death is a two-way street that offers its ups and downs for both parties, no matter what side of the Veil they're on. So, and I'm sorry if this upsets you, but they also witness the jealousy, fear and greed that manifests when there's a healthy estate left to divide, as well as the underhanded behaviour, hidden agendas and the mind games people play in a bid to influence, manipulate and gain favour with those responsible for the distribution of funds, valuables and property. And while we think of our deceased loved ones being negatively affected by the antics of those left behind, along with the raw emotion, grief and emotional desperation that rises to the surface, it's important to remember that what we do and how we respond during times like that is often a reflection of our environment, our family dynamics and the manner in which our family (referring here to the one that has passed away) has handled situations and circumstances that may have come up when they were alive. For example, if the child of the one who has died was spoilt, or their bad behaviour was constantly overlooked because it was too late to do anything about, was excused for vague or obscure reasons or pardoned without consequence because of past experiences or events that the parent deemed responsible for their child's behaviour, then how that child behaves at their parent's funeral is as much as the child's 'fault' as it is the parent's. In turn, for parents to be forced to watch their child's bad behaviour from the Spirit World is just as important for the parent's ultimate journey and the evolution of their soul as it is for the child, who will one day be forced to face the karmic consequence of their own life choices before deciding whether to acknowledge them or not.

It's interesting to note that there are certain traditional flowers that are offered as tributes when someone passes: carnations, – their name has ancient roots in the terms incarnate and reincarnation; chrysanthemums – mainly because their name includes the word Mum marking them deeply with emotional connotation; roses – traditionally associated with love, promise and heartfelt pledges; lilies (also known as death lilies) – which symbolise innocence restored; and gladiolus – from gladius meaning sword, named after the Roman gladiators and symbolise integrity, honour and truth.

The grave

Providing a place to visit the dead, to continue our goodbyes and to sit with their memory in times of hardship, when we may have once called them on the telephone or visited their home to seek comfort or their counsel, is the grave or burial site where the ashes or body of the deceased have been laid to rest. I used to think it strange that someone would choose to visit a cemetery, to sit on or beside a gravestone and spend time in silence with someone who was no longer physically there. But I've since realised, after losing people I love, that the grave or memorial site isn't just a plot of land or a hole in a wall.

After we offer up our loved ones to Great Spirit, their coffin or casket becomes a vehicle that symbolically provides safe passage to the Other Realms, while their final resting place becomes a sacred site, holding memory and wisdom. Sacred too becomes their skeletal remains, which hold ancestral connection, spiritual lineage and family history, while their flesh (or their ashes if they were cremated and not buried), as it slowly returns to the earth, becomes the 'power of seed' (which I write about later on page 145), offering a permanent record of their precious time spent on Earth. When we see the burial site as sacred, we begin to see it as a portal through which to extend our awareness, to vision quest, seek healing and to find answers to questions that allude human consciousness. Like the faerie mounds or ancient cairns, kurgans or barrows of Irish tradition, the graves of our beloved hold potential to become 'tomb-wombs', or personal places of rebirth, offering opportunity to start over, have prayers heard and our wishes granted.

Getting Dead

I used to fear death. It wasn't that I was afraid of not being here anymore, but I was afraid of 'getting dead'. Not so much the idea of dying ... but rather the 'how' I was destined to get dead. Would it hurt? Would I know? Would I be scared? And what would it be like to be dead? I remember as a child hearing on television reports that it had been prophesised the world would end on a certain date and consequently not being able to sleep leading up to that date, but then waking the next day feeling relieved to know I was still alive.

I think it scares a lot of people as the unknown often does. It wasn't until my two friends died in the car accident that I finally found a sense of peace with the processes of death and dying. The car was split in half, and the boys were killed instantly. Whether he can be considered fortunate or not is not for me to say, but the driver escaped without any lasting physical injuries. When asked how he had managed to get himself out of the twisted wreck, he described a 'white lady riding a white horse' who had guided him out with the light from a torch. The police searched for the white lady for weeks after, to no avail. I had my own theories on who that white lady was but when I tried to explain it to the officers in attendance, they dismissed my ramblings as someone in shock. It was a horrible accident, and the emotional devastation it caused that night and the years following was unbearable. Wondering why the boys were taking so long to return, I stumbled across the accident as I went looking for them, just after the police had. After explaining who I was, I accompanied them to inform their parents of the accident and, to this day, their heart-breaking cries of despair on hearing the news still haunts my soul. While I remember losing any remnant of faith in God I had held on to from childhood, I found I wasn't so afraid of death anymore because I supposed, 'If you guys can do it, I can too'. Instead of actioning a fleeting thought to join them that night, though, I made a pact to explore the world we journey to after we leave this one, and to learn as much as I could about what life was like in the Afterworld.

After the boys died, I had many vivid dreams in which they would visit me and tell me things. They would share their experiences of the Afterworld with me, including what they were doing and how our future interactions would look like and why. One of the most profound revelations was how they had come to find themselves on the Other Side and how – looking back – their transition was far more painful for those of us left behind than it was for them to physically go through it. In the dreams, I could clearly see them in the car: the youngest in the back, his older brother in the front passenger seat. They were laughing and enjoying the ride. Suddenly, at the same time, they both look out the left-hand side window of the car to see a large, heavy-set wooden door set among the trees. The door was slightly ajar, and light spilled out onto the roadside. The urge to go through it, they told me, was far beyond their control and the next thing they knew they were walking through a park of sorts, with the sound of a violent car crash fading away in the distance. It took them a while to realise they were no longer in the car, but once realisation struck, they explained it was too late to change their minds making it impossible to return to the physical world to deal with the crippling consequences. By moving through the numinous door, they had little choice but to leave their physical bodies behind. Being that they – as are all human bodies – were a complex combination of matter and gas, there was no hope of them passing through the subtle Veil separating the Afterworld from ours and, as a result, were found a short while later in the crumpled wreck of the car.

Once they'd found themselves in the Afterworld, the boys had effectively stepped off the Good Red Road of Life and had embarked on an entirely new adventure; this one taking them along a very long path known as the Good Blue Road of Spirit, or the Road of Spirit. This path would lead them directly to the Creator, but along the way, they've since told me, they faced various challenges and lessons and met many folk; some of whom were originally from our world and others who were not.

I remember sitting with another beloved friend as she neared the end of her life. She had lived a passionate life and was loved and respected by all as a brave, outspoken and inspirational woman. Her breathing had been laboured leading up to her last hours, and she hadn't moved a muscle in what seemed like ages. Her arms rested at her sides, her eyes were shut and her mouth expressionless. She was struggling, and we knew her time to leave us was approaching. I remember going out to the small lounge area where friends and family had gathered, my wife and young son among them. As I walked into the room, my son – who was all of three at the time – pointed to a couch where my friend's future father-in-law was seated. The space on the couch next to him was empty – or so it appeared to us. Squealing with delight, my son indicated toward the couch and exclaimed: 'Two dads!' He said it two more times before pointing at the empty space and then the gentleman seated on the couch and, looking at me, shouted one last time: 'Two dads'. The look on his face was one of amazement and joy and with that, the room went silent. Everyone looked at the empty space on the couch and in an emotional whisper, one of the women present said, 'We were just wondering if her grandfather [who had passed several years before] would come for her'.

Returning to my friend's hospital room, I was relieved to hear that her breathing had eased and that she sounded more peaceful. I remember telling her I loved her and reminded her she'd always been my favourite. I loved her family as my own, but it had always been a private joke between us that out of everyone, she was my favourite. She was like a sister and the thought of losing her was almost too much to contemplate. But lose her I did, and I will never forget the moments leading up to when it happened. She hadn't opened her eyes or moved her arms in – I want to say days – but in truth, it was probably only several hours. But during those last few minutes, she lifted her hand and placed it on her chest. She then opened her eyes, but instead of focusing her gaze on any of us, she looked past us – way past us – and... smiled! A beautiful, heartfelt, genuine, deeply meaningful smile. But it was meant for someone else. Someone standing behind us. None of us dared to look or move. Instead, with tears streaming down our cheeks, we focused our gaze on her and relished in the happiness and joy she was obviously experiencing. And then someone in the room whispered, 'Her grandfather is here', and we all started to cry. As her smile faded, she closed her eyes and we assumed that was that. But then, the second miracle happened. She opened her eyes again, stared past us one more time and gave an even bigger smile than the one before. We all gasped and cried some more. Whoever had appeared this time was even more loved than those who had appeared to her before. We all agreed that, 'Her grandfather is indeed with her now', and we knew this to be true because of all the people she had loved, her grandfather was her ultimate hero. And then her breathing stopped, her smile dropped away, and we knew she had gone. Forever. She had up and left us. And with that, we fell into each other's arms and sobbed and sobbed and sobbed...

After a while, we focused our attention on my dear friend whose lifeless form lay – for the first time in ages – in a genuine state of rest. She had been so sick for so long, during which time she had endured incredible suffering and pain, and to know she was finally at peace gave us some degree of consolation. But to our delight, she had one last miracle in store for us – her smile had returned. I kid you not! A huge smile was spread across her face, and it was still there when the hospital staff arrived to confirm her passing and when the funeral director arrived to take her body to the funeral parlour. 'Did you put that smile on her face?' they quizzed us, to which we vehemently denied any interference. We wondered how that would be possible, and then we realised they were asking if we'd physically pushed the corners of her mouth upward to create a smile, the very thought of which horrified us! 'No,' we exclaimed, shocked, 'she did it herself.' They replied in wonder, 'We've never seen anything like this before'. She looked very peaceful, as if she'd fallen asleep and was enjoying a dream that made her happy to the core.

After losing people I dearly loved and witnessing their passing in intimate ways, I can't help but wonder whether, no matter how violent, tragic, cruel or unfair death may look or feel to those left behind, the actual process of dying is somehow cushioned or cocooned in some sort of protective and sacred energy outside our realm of conscious understanding so that the entire procedure, from the onset, is peaceful.

Years of watching wildlife documentaries has seen me formulate a theory that when a prey animal realises the predator chasing it is going to win, it surrenders control and 'dies' to the physical world seconds before the hunter has a chance to deliver its fatal blow. Similarly, even if the lead-up to the last breath is frightening or traumatic for the individual in question (which the process of dying can be for some folk), I like to believe that once the human soul realises what is happening and it accepts the inevitable and surrenders control, any pain or fear felt consciously or physically is fleeting – even if the heart is beating and the brain is active at the time of death. I also believe that seconds before this lead-up, the journey to the Afterworld has inherently begun and the Angels on the other side are already there, waiting to receive them.

Who is Death?

Besides the worry of how 'getting dead' may look and feel, the only other thing that I used to worry about was what Death would be like and by that, I mean I wondered what Death 'the being' would be like. When I was younger, I held the worry that the old images of Death may be true; that he wore a black hooded robe that only half-concealed his skeletal head, while carrying a razor-sharp scythe used to drag the souls of the departed to the Other Place. The whole notion freaked me out, to say the least.

Now that I'm older, I hold the belief that if you think Death looks like the stereotyped figure we've been indoctrinated with, then there's a big chance that is exactly what Death will look like when he 'comes for you'. I wonder if this dark perception of Death is instilled by fear; fear that comes with the inner knowing that you may not have been the most savoury type of person or that you consciously lived your life doing wrong to yourself and others, and the dread that something bigger than us may be waiting after death to judge and punish us for our poor life choices and behaviour.

When we are fit, healthy and living life to the fullest, we tend to believe we will be around forever and we don't give any real thought for what may happen after life until our time on Earth looks like it's about to end. We tend to live for the moment, without any consideration of karma or what happens next. So, if our life is lived with a lack of consideration, empathy or respect for others, the process of dying may be more confronting than it may be for those who have lived their life in a mindful manner, paying attention to how their actions impact others. For these individuals, Death may present himself as a judger, tormenter or a punisher of souls. Or perhaps that is how he may be perceived until they have made their way to the Afterworld, and the process of addressing and acknowledging the life they lived has commenced and after which Death may show himself (or herself) in a totally different way.

For the majority, however, I believe Death appears as someone or something familiar; a loved one who has crossed over before us, a beloved pet, a Guide, an Angel or some other non-threatening yet acquainted energy that fills our heart with happiness and bliss the moment we lay eyes upon it.

The Light

When my friends were killed in the car accident, I couldn't help but put a night-light in the coffin leading up to the funeral of the youngest knowing that, while alive, he had harboured a fear of the dark. The last thing I wanted was for him to reach the Afterworld and find it was dark there. I looked upon the move as a 'better to be safe than sorry' act so that I (and he) could rest easy, just in case. In my heart of hearts, I believed that if 'going to the light' meant just that, there would be no chance of it being dark there but my Virgoan mind was so full of doubt and questions that I had to be sure. So many people make the comment that it's 'lights out' when you die, so I wanted to eliminate any chance of it being dark there when the boys arrived. Obviously, the likelihood of the night-light serving any real, practical use to a disembodied spirit was zero. The act of placing the plug-in light carried symbolic and emotional significance which, I believe, supported me through the grieving process more than it advantaged them.

Sure, science will tell you that the burst or tunnel of white light people describe just before the point of death – reported by those who have been resuscitated and who've had an NDE (near-death experience) or who, while being monitored by medical staff, remain fully conscious despite appearing to be asleep with no blood pressure but then die soon after the energetic surge was recorded – is caused by a torrent of brain activity triggered by a rush of electrical impulses from the brain when the inflow of oxygen stops, resulting in vivid visions and what is typically described afterward as a spiritual experience. While all this makes perfect sense, and is logical when you stop and think about it, it only explains the science behind what may be happening to the brain and doesn't explain the spiritual experiences survivors report about and why the visions they have oftentimes include visitations by deceased loved ones and Angels, with glimpses of paradise-like landscapes they have never visited or seen before.

I can accept that white light and random visions or sensations may affect the mind and body at the point of death, but how can it be that the visions are so often very specific and personal to the one facing death? How can it be that these people often come back from the brink with clear messages or otherworldly words of love they've had the sense of hearing while in the indeterminate state? While science probably also has answers for these questions, I believe that after this life we experience an afterlife, and that after this world we journey to what can only be described as an Afterworld that is known by many names to different people. I also believe the burst or tunnel of white light we experience before entering the Afterworld is the door or Veil our spirit must pass through as we transcend this physical existence and enter the next. And just as we may walk along a track at night with the light of the moon or the overhanging streetlamps brightening our path, the white light we experience when leaving this Earthly Plane may be the illuminating, welcoming and inherently familiar essence of pure love that reaches out from beyond the Veil, while the beings we witness are those that have come or who have been sent to guide us home along the Good Blue Road of Spirit. Either way, I believe that an indispensable portion of a person's spirit or consciousness endures after the death of their body, and my belief is apparently supported by a universal concept of an afterlife that is recognised by people, faiths and cultures all over the world.

Heaven

The English word we know today as Heaven is a modern derivative of the earlier 'heven', which has roots in the even earlier 'heofon', a word that once meant 'sky, firmament'

(firmament referring to a dense, translucent casing that domed Earth, protecting it from the 'waters' above) but eventually came to reference the Christianised 'where God lives'.

Heaven is commonly explained by many faiths and religions as a spiritual, astral or unequalled place inhabited by beings such as gods, goddesses, Angels, Jinn, saints, spirits and ancestors and described as a place existing on a higher plane or being more virtuous than Earth – a holy or utopian place, a divine paradise or nirvana.

Considered more a state of existence rather than an actual place located somewhere in the Universe, traditional Christian faith, to a large degree, metaphorically views Heaven as existing in 'the sky', housing the Throne of God and all the Holy Angels, as well as being the temporary resting place of all the converted souls of the dead before their resurrection and eventual return to Earth. Some Christians believe that in the Afterworld, those who embrace God reside in mansions of different kinds, some of which are found in the heavens or in paradise and in a place loosely referred to as 'the City'.

Similarly, the Bahá'í Faith, a religion founded in Iran that espouses the importance of all religions and celebrates the equality of all people, embraces the concept of Heaven as a 'spiritual condition' or being close to God, with the notion of Hell obviously reflecting the opposite. According to this faith, while life in the Afterworld is incomprehensible for those still on the physical plane, they firmly believe that the Afterworld is a place of great joy but is as different to this world as this world is as different to that of a child's that's still developing in its mother's womb. For Bahá'ís, peace in this world can be found in the knowledge that the identity and consciousness of their dearly departed is retained after death and that these spirits can remember the physical lives they lived, and recognise and talk to the spirits of those they knew in life.

Here in Australia, beliefs that were and are still shared by many Indigenous Australian people centre on the notion of the Afterworld, with details varying from one nation or language group to the next. How a person lived their life, for example, had no impact on how their spirit was received or treated in the Afterworld, or the Eternal Dreaming as it was also called, being that there was no recognised Heaven or Hell. The only factors determining whether a spirit made it to the Afterworld were if the dead displayed bodily signs of participating in certain ceremonial rites before death, and whether the bereaved carried out their funerary rites correctly. The human spirit was believed to be everlasting, with the identity of the deceased person lasting but a short time after death. While it could be said that the limited continuance of the dead's identity meant the eventual expiry of the spirit, nothing could have been further from the truth, with the process essentially marking the spirit as immortal, ongoing and everlasting, even if the notion of reincarnation was not recognised as part of its journey.

But according to Buddhism several heavens exist, all of which are of an illusionary reality, or *samsara*. People who accrue good karma may find themselves reborn into one of these heavens, with their time there considered temporary because their good karma is gradually used up. Once their good karma is depleted, they may be reborn once again into another realm, perhaps as a person, an animal or something else. Being that the Universe is transitory, Buddhists believe that our world is just one of many realms or paths that we can follow. So, with the understanding that Heaven is impermanent and part of *samsara*, Buddhists live their life on Earth in such a way as to hopefully avoid the process of rebirth by attaining enlightenment, or nirvana, which is not a heaven but a state of mind.

The Ancient Egyptians had very specific believes surrounding death and the afterlife. They believed, for example, that humans possessed a life force called the *ka*, that left the body when the person died. During life, the *ka* was sustained with the consumption of food and drink, so naturally it was assumed that for the *ka* to survive after death, it must continue to eat and drink, even if the essence of what it was offered was all it could consume. Besides the *ka*, people were also believed to have a *ba*, which embodied their unique set of essential spiritual traits and qualities. Unlike the *ka*, the *ba* was said to remain with the body after death but that after specific funerary rites, the *ba* could be released from the body to be reunited with the *ka* to live on as an *akh*. However, for the *ba* to live outside the body as an *akh*, it was essential for the body to be embalmed because it was believed the *ba* returned to the body at night for nourishment. At first, it was believed that only Pharaohs had a *ba*, and only they could ascend to the sky to live among the stars in the company of the gods. When a commoner died, it was believed that without a *ba* they moved to a shadowy, miserable land where existence was the opposite to life. Over time, beliefs changed, and the Egyptians began to accept that everyone had a *ba*, and that the journey to the afterlife was not just restricted to those of royal blood. But with the change came a new belief that saw the soul forced to pass several spiritual tests before the final judgement known as the 'weighing of the heart'. During the weighing of the heart, the gods gathered to judge the deeds and actions of the deceased during their life and, if they determined the deceased to be worthy, their *ka* and *ba* were united and allowed to live on as an *akh*. While the *akhs* of Pharaohs and those of noble blood were said to exist alongside Ra (the Sun God – king of all gods in Ancient Egypt), the *akhs* of everyday folk lived on in the Land of Osiris, a beautiful utopian realm located somewhere in the Underworld.

According to Greek mythology, flowing into the Underworld from the physical plane exist five mystical rivers: the first being the river Styx, also known as the river of hatred that circles the Underworld seven times. The second is the river Acheron, or the river of pain across which Charon the Ferryman rows the dead across (although some stories say he traverses the river Styx, or both). Next is the river Lethe, or the river of forgetfulness, followed by the river Phlegethon, the river of fire, the river Cocytus, the river of wailing and the river Oceanus, the river that encircles the world and marks the east edge of the Underworld. The concept of Charon is what is known as a psychopomp or a 'guide of souls'; an animal, spirit, Angel or deity whose role it was to escort the newly deceased from Earth and provide safe passage to the Afterworld. It was not their responsibility to judge the deceased but to simply deliver them into the realm of the dead. And as a guide of souls, Charon's role was to escort the deceased across rivers Styx and Acheron that separated the physical world from the Afterworld, a service recompensed with a single coin that was placed in the mouth of the dead before their funeral.

Also known as the Underworld is Hell, or the Lower World or the Low Place. Hell, according to many religions and belief systems, is an actual place or a perpetual state of suffering and castigation a person who has lived a less than desirable life may find themselves in after death. Some religions view the concept of Hell as an eternal endpoint, while others view it as more of a transitional stage endured between incarnations, but it is mostly described as being located elsewhere, in a lower dimension or deep within Earth itself. Other religions that do not recognise a Heaven or Hell or view the Afterworld as being place of suffering or joy, view Hell (also known as Sheol or Hades) as being nothing more than the home of the dead, the tomb or an impartial place located within Earth.

I personally do not hold any opinion or belief in a Hellworld, and prefer to acknowledge Hel, who I believe this realm was erroneously named after. In Norse mythology, Hel was said to have presided over an Underworld kingdom of the same name, where she welcomed those who had failed to die a heroic or distinguished death. Described as a daughter of Loki, Hel was apparently selected by the god Odin to govern the realm, located in Niflheim. Niflheim, one of two primeval realms, was a world of freezing water, ice and cold. The other, Muspelheim, was a realm of fire. Between these realms of cold and heat was Hel, a mist-filled world where creation began after its waters mixed with the heat of Muspelheim to form a world of 'creating steam'. Because she was said to receive the dead, the expression 'go to Hel' simply meant 'to die'. With distinct blue-coloured skin and a cheerless appearance, Hel's kingdom was not a place of eternal misery or punishment, with no hint of fire or brimstone. Instead, she ruled massive mansions and had many servants and loyal followers where the dead lived a good life.

If Heaven can indeed be described as a physical place that one goes to after death, then I've always envisioned it as a green, lush kingdom, thick with looming mountains, ancient rainforests and a wild coastline and deep valleys riddled with intricate tunnels and underground temples overshadowed by cliff-clinging cities of stone and twisted vine. The land in Heaven is rich and it isn't simply fertile – it's ALIVE; alive with audible, visible, tangible energies. It's alive with the force of the Creator Spirit. It literally pulsates with memories of ancient times, the promise of experience and of palpable wisdom. The land isn't just rich with crystals, for example, it's alive with their life force, their spirit and the divas that manifest their power. The land there isn't just abundant with unique animals and birds; it's ALIVE with their PRESENCE – their medicine, their power, and their connection to the physical world, the Earth Mother herself. The flowers sing their ballads of healing potential, the trees remember their birth, their wisdom and their might, and as their tap roots reach down, anchoring Heaven to Earth, the people that dwell there live in harmony with one another and the essence of all things. For me, the concept of Heaven is comparable to the Buddhist **Shambhala**, a Pure Land; a kingdom that's as close as is humanly conceivable to the notion of a truly utopian realm that has an existence which is as mystical or spiritual as it is physical or earthly.

One version of Heaven that I've always felt comfortable accepting as a truth is the idea of the Summerland, a term synonymous with both the Wiccan (as opposed to Witchcraft, which can be described as a practice rather than a religion) and Neopagan religious movements. The Summerland is an etheric realm of pondering and remembering, where we reunite and communicate with the spirits of deceased loved ones and where our spirit can stop and rest in between physical incarnations. While it is commonly believed that the spirit retains little if any memory of being in the Summerland once it reincarnates on the mortal plane, some believe that when an individual vows to live their life to the fullest they finally reach a point after many lifetimes where they can honestly say that they totally comprehend and appreciate every facet and sentiment of physical human existence, and when petitioned, the god or goddess they pray to above all others will grant them permission to remain in the Summerland for an eternity. What I love most about the notion of the Summerland is that it is portrayed as being a place of peace and extreme beauty, where everything we hold dear is upheld to its richest potential and where, like the concept of Elysium or the Elysian Fields (an ancient Greek version of the Afterworld that mainly welcomed the mortal offspring of gods or other heroes), an individual could live an eternal, blessed and happy life after their death, indulging in the same pleasures they enjoyed in life. And like the Elysian Fields, the Summerland is said to offer endless blue skies, crystal-clear streams, lakes and waterfalls, rolling green meadows of lush grass, wild flowers and gently undulating hills. Everyone is welcome in the Summerland, including those considered bad or evil, because the point of going to the Summerland is to assess your life, to process the lessons we've learned and to heal from pain, suffering and hardship and to plan how we can live a better life when we return. During this time, we can decide when it's time for us to reincarnate, how our next life will pan out, what conditions we may face and whether we will be a man or a woman – or something else.

The Veil

Like a house has walls that separate one room from another, so too are etheric walls designed to separate one realm of consciousness from the next. And the reason for the walls is that without them the worlds would begin to spill and overflow into one another and cause chaos, confusion and imbalance. Their purpose is to maintain a sense of order because without order the Universe would literally begin to fray at the seams and, like a house built from cards, would collapse at the slightest bump. The difference between the walls that separate the rooms in a house and those that separate the worlds, however, is that the world-separating walls are as thin as they are dense. As confusing as that may sound, the fact is these walls are not physical but etheric, which means they're both intangible and impenetrable. Supporters of the 'many worlds' or 'meta-universe' interpretation (a theory that hypothesises a set of worlds existing side by side, in diverse dimensions of which ours is one) and even scientists who suggest the existence of a dimension of non-local quantum reality or an invisible layer of quantum reality, agree that a 'world' of sorts seems to exist and that essentially acts as a kind of protective barrier or buffer zone between Great Spirit and the world of matter (our Earth Plane). But putting science aside, if we are to simply believe what we were taught at Sunday School, apart from our physical world there exists another realm that inhabits a higher or spiritual plane of reality, and separating the two is a veil of energy that allows the two worlds to interact, while simultaneously keeping them entirely separate from one another. One of the worlds (ours) is made up of matter, while the other (the Afterworld) is constituted entirely of Spirit.

PART TWO

The Good Blue Road of Spirit

There are many theories that try to explain or map the journey of the spirit as it navigates the Good Blue Road of Spirit to the Afterworld. Unless you've personally taken this journey yourself and returned with clear memory, no one can know for sure what the journey entails from start to finish. All we can do is garner our own thoughts, feelings and ideas, collate stories and accounts offered by others, and splice them together, like the pieces of a jigsaw, to create a whole-picture scenario that offers some sort of consistent, plausible and emotional comfort.

I plan to outline two scenarios that help to map the journey the spirit takes on its way to the Afterworld; both of which have afforded me a sense of peace over the years.

I choose to outline them separately because they were explained to me by two different spiritual sources, with the second scenario holding greater personal significance to me. Although the first one is more widely accepted by spiritual teachers and those who study the notion of the afterlife, for me it tends to overlook some of the details my own scenario explores and explains. But to honour both, I will first outline the more traditional and broadly accepted journey before I summarise my own version of the journey I believe the spirit takes before finding itself in the Afterworld.

I'm sure you'll agree that the journey along the Good Blue Road of Spirit to the Afterworld must begin with death, when the person's physical body dies to the physical world. This first leg of the journey is like entering the ground floor of a spiritual hotel; the lobby of sorts, otherwise known as the physical universe or the Earth Plane.

Journey to the Afterworld – a popular explanation

On the second floor, or the second leg of the journey, the first of these two scenarios can be explored. And it's here that the spirit of the departed enters the 'Earthbound' chapter (also known as the Astral Plane) when directly after death, the person's spirit may realise they're no longer confined to their physical body and may experience an 'out of body' sensation where they find themselves floating above their body, looking down upon it. And it's while in this state (sometime after the body has gone through some sort of funerary right) that living people with 'the sight' (psychics and mediums) are able to communicate with the spirit of the departed, despite the departed being invisible to those still living.

It's during this chapter of the journey too, that the Earth-bound may not realise they've died and may become confused as to why they are sometimes able to still see the living, while at other times they can't (a notion explored in the 2001 award-winning Spanish-American supernatural gothic horror film *The Others*, starring Nicole Kidman).

The third floor of the spiritual hotel, or the third leg of the journey, is where the person's spirit enters what is known as the Void; a silent, timeless stage enveloped in complete darkness – not a sinister, looming darkness, but rather a protective, nourishing, womblike darkness, where we dream, contemplate and process. The Void is empty of all things, except love, the light found within and the thoughts and emotions of those that find themselves there.

After the Void, the person's spirit faces a fourth leg of their journey, where it's almost sucked into portal of sorts and rushed through a tunnel at some speed toward a radiant, pure white light. Sometimes this chapter is shared with other spirits undertaking their own journey, but oftentimes it is taken alone.

The fifth floor of the spiritual hotel might be described as a kind of waiting room, where the person's spirit may recognise and communicate with the spirits of deceased friends, family and associates. It is here that it may meet the Council of Elders; a collective of Ascended Teachers and Masters, said to be the spirits of esteemed spiritual leaders many of us have looked up to during life. It is here too, that it may be reminded of things it has forgotten from lives lived in the past. Incidentally, it is at this point that those who have experienced a near-death experience have been told it's not their time to die and have been returned to the Earth Plane.

If this description is to be believed, then perhaps it was on this plane that my two friends killed in the car accident were at when they came to visit me in a very clear vision-like dream not long after they had passed. I was boarding a train, and as I entered the carriage, I saw a (still living) friend of the brothers sitting on the bench seat opposite the door. I remember asking him, 'Hi! What are you doing here?' to which he replied, 'I think you're here to see them.' He pointed to the other side of the carriage that was out of my range of view. As the train started to pull away from the station, I stepped fully into the carriage and turned to see the boys sitting side by side; the younger of the two wearing the same face covering he had been buried with – a lace cloth hiding the injuries he had acquired during the accident. I asked how they were doing and told them we all missed them dearly. They told me they were 'on their way' and that once settled, they'd come and visit me soon. I indicated toward their friend on the opposite side of the carriage with a questioning look who, on second glance, no longer resembled the person I first recognised him to be. They replied, 'Oh, he's here to take care of us'. And then they told me they had to go, that I had to disembark at the next stop but to know they were okay – and that's when I woke up.

It's after this leg of the journey that some spiritualists believe the person's spirit now finds itself on the sixth floor of the spiritual hotel, or the chapter that sees it delivered into a realm that's ruled by certain Soul Groups and influenced by, not including Earth, the various planetary energies of our solar system. It is said that it is here the human spirit incarnates through many spirit levels between its earthly lives until it has reached a suitable growth ranking before it's able to access the higher floors of the spiritual hotel. It's like it's required to earn an appropriate number of points before being given the security pass to venture to the next floor and, the ultimate prize, the penthouse. The various points may be earned by dealing with emotional issue experienced during their most recent earthly incarnation, through to facing mental and karmic memories and addressing old desires, needs and wants. Some spiritualists believe that it's here on this spirit level that the deceased gather in Soul Groups linked to past family ties, friendships and even interests, where they're watched over, guided and supported by other older spirits that have decided to stay here and to adopt this responsibility as part of their growth.

The next (and second last) floor of the spiritual hotel is like a world unto itself; a galaxy-like world riddled with stars sometimes referred to as the City of Stars or the Kingdom of Light. It's here, on this final leg of the journey, that the person's spirit may come face to face with its higher self and finally begin to realise that it has have finally earned the right to advance to the eighth and final floor of the spiritual hotel. This floor is essentially the penthouse suite, and the definitive destination of the Good Blue Road of Spirit. This is the ultimate echelon that all spirits work hard to attain and is, of course, the Afterworld.

I remember having these 'soul levels' explained to me

when I used to sit in spiritual development circles as a young student, and while many facets of what I was taught rang true, there were equally as many aspects that didn't. And while it is tempting for me to specify the aspects that didn't, I've opted to let you decide for yourself. But what I took away from these tutorial-style teachings and what I learned during my apprenticeship under the Elder and later dedicated myself to, forms the basis for the second scenario of the United Element's journey that I would like to now share with you.

Journey to the Afterworld – The Author's Interpretation

The soul, the spirit and the United Element

I used to view the notion of 'Mind, Body, Soul' as referring to the **mind**: our intellect, personality, character, value and beliefs, our longing for evidence or proof, and our human need to know, understand, learn and control the outcome of any situation, the **body**: the essence of love and intimacy and what makes us 'mortal', breakable or frail, while reminding us how precious life really is, and the **soul**: which I thought was the same thing as the spirit, both of which somehow suggested or even promised life everlasting or 'immortality'.

And while this remains largely true for me, and this is just my personal belief, I've come to realise that there is a big difference between the soul and the spirit. A soul, put simply, can be used to indicate a living person or animal, or how the person or animal chooses to live their life. We have all used the expression: 'What a beautiful soul' when referring to an empathetic, kind or loving person, or: 'You're an old (or wise) soul' when describing a baby that seems to emit an unusually heightened sense of aware- ness. And it's not uncommon to refer to someone that everyone agrees 'wouldn't hurt a soul' as being a 'gentle soul' or a 'kind-hearted soul'. When someone seems to lose their way in life, we may describe them as being 'a lost soul' or a 'poor soul', and when someone's health is failing, we may say they have a 'weakened soul' or a 'tired soul'. It's also a common thing to reference a living person as 'a mortal soul', which suggests the soul is not everlasting and is susceptible to death.

On the other hand, the spirit is best described as force or life force, manna, breath or energy. Without a spirit, a person is dead. When someone dies, for example, we may say 'we felt (or saw) their spirit leave', or when someone teeters on the brink of death but is saved, or experiences a near-death-experience, they may be described as having 'their breath (or spirit) almost sucked out of them'. When describing a passionate person or wilful animal, we may refer to them as 'bursting with energy', 'spirited', or 'full of life', which essentially means the same thing. In short, spirit or 'the spark of life' refers to the intangible force that gives life to all living things. It can be compared to the battery that charges a radio or the electrical surge that starts a car engine and, like electricity, the spirit is not sentient and is devoid of emotion, but without it our body would die. It is after death, though, that the soul or what makes us who we are (our identity, personality and character) and the spirit (our life force) do something few would expect.

I believe that when someone dies, a residual portion or the vitality of their soul (*ba*) (as per the Ancient Egyptian's version) is reduced to a blue print; a summarised, vibrational seed that holds true everything that made that person them. It's like their personality, character, values and beliefs are condensed and downloaded into a dossier of basic facts that essentially merges, as a secondary or tributary facet, with the person's spirit (*ka*) to create a new element (*akh*). Incidentally, in my opinion, this 'new' element has always been the elusive fifth element, the fifth force that single-handedly unites and harnesses the elements of air, fire, water and earth to create life. Once combined with the spirit, the soul becomes nothing more than a dormant record, holding no life force of its own, offering the spirit no nourishment or advantage other than inherently reminding it of the nature of the person the spirit once served. Without the spirit acting as a host of sorts, the soul would cease to exist, but without the soul the spirit would continue, holding no memory of the person it previously belonged to marking it eternal with no thought of resurrection.

Soon after death (perhaps after the mourners have offered their funerary rites or a certain amount of time has passed, and the dead has had time to recover or heal, depending on how they died and under what circumstance) I believe the new element splits or divides into three portions. To be clear, it doesn't so much separate into three equal parts, but rather clones itself into three equal wholes. The three are independent of one another, while always remaining united as a single, United Element.

It is my belief that these three 'wholes' then part ways to embark on their own separate journeys; three separate journeys undertaken simultaneously that will see them sharing a single experience of the Other Realms, so that when they eventually reunite, the memory of their travels will be one, with nothing left to do but reincarnate and do it all over again.

The Astral Plane

The first third of the United Element's journey is a short one because it doesn't go anywhere at all, but instead remains Earthbound on the Astral Plane with the living. It stays here with us knowingly and willingly, and is by no means trapped or confined to our Earth realm against its will. No matter how hard someone may try to 'send them to the light', it won't make a scrap of difference because choice and free will gives it the right to be here. This aspect of the United Element stays here to lovingly watch, observe and guide those it knew and loved while living, while almost going about its business as if it was still alive. In saying that though, the ability to go about it's business as if it was still alive comes with some limitations because, if in life the United Element had responsibilities such as a spouse and children but chose to live a selfish life without consideration for their wellbeing or upkeep, then it wouldn't be allowed to continue to live on in the Astral Plane in the same way. Instead, it would be required to see, feel and show accountability for its choices and to inherently carry the knowledge and consequence of its behaviour until later in its journey when it'd be given opportunity to put things right.

Putting this aside for now, the fact that our loved ones remain on the Earthbound Plane is, for me, the primary reason we can still 'see' them on occasion and sense them watching or interacting with us (often by reminding us of their familiar scent, or by manifesting miraculous 'ah-ha' moments of realisation that leave no room for doubt for those experiencing them) and why psychics and mediums are able to tap into them and pass messages of love to us 'from the other side' long after their death, and – based on these messages – why our loved ones seem to know what we're doing at any given time. I believe that this aspect of the United Element willingly remains Earthbound for up to seven generations and stays close to its core circle of family and friends until they have all made the transition to the other side in their own time and in individual ways.

The Underworld

The second third of the United Element journey takes it to the Underworld: a restful, dream-like, star-lit realm of darkness, stillness and peace, not dissimilar to the world it started its life journey in – the womb. Despite being blanketed in total darkness; the Underworld is neither gloomy or depressing. Instead, it's a place of enlighten-ment and beauty, realisation and remembrance that's illuminated by the purest expression of peace and love.

It's here in the Underworld that the United Element is given the opportunity to ponder and reflect and to come to terms with its life and how it lived it, and how its choices and behaviour affected and influenced those still living. It's here that the United Element realises the mistakes it made during life, and the full impact or consequences of those mistakes while making any changes of attitude and improving its approach to life, while deciding what to shun when it next incarnates to ensure a better life for all, such as the need to control others, possess material things, show loyalty to unhelpful associates, harbour trapped or outworn emotions and other unessentials such as anger, resentment, jealousy and greed. It's here that the United Element realises the need to leave its old life behind and essentially undergoes a second death of sorts; the death of its familiar self which will, in time, allow for the emergence of its true self. Death is, after all, never a permanent state of being but rather an opportunity to transition from what may have been an old, tired, unwholesome way of living to embrace what could be a new, healthy, more fruitful one.

As previously discussed, the ancient Egyptians believed they would be judged on their actions during life before being granted access to the Afterworld. I believe that it's in the Underworld that this weighing of the heart ceremony takes place. Those who may have committed atrocious or violent crimes such as murder, rape and sexually based crimes against children are 'held' until they show accountability for their crimes, show remorse or repent, and do what needs to be done to ensure the likelihood to reoffend next time around is eliminated from their consciousness and no longer poses a threat. They cannot leave, proceed or reunite with the other aspects of their United Element until all three have in a cohesive manner done enough to appease and reassure the Angels, Ascended Teachers and Spirit Guides that work and speak on behalf of Great Spirit/Creator that the United Element has indeed rehabilitated. If no such assurance can be offered, then the United Element will remain in the Underworld – with all three aspects literally held in limbo in their respective allocated realms – for as long as it takes, and so it will remain until the end of days...

It's in the Underworld that the United Element is faced with certain challenges or opportunities designed to test its resolve. One such 'test' is the pouring of the Waters of

Life from two jugs that represent the marriage of the two opposites that are inherently equal, the yin and the yang, the feminine and the masculine. The choice is whether to empty the jugs into the first of three pools the United Element will encounter while in the Underworld and which represents the subconscious or Creation, or onto the dry land, which is symbolic of the material world. Either act could be the right choice, and equally, both would offer consequences and the opportunity to rethink. However, the decision to return the water from one jug to the pool while emptying the other onto the land indicates a desire to renew both, while reminding the United Element that nothing in life is ever truly lost.

The second pool the United Element will come across is the Pool of Memories, which offers the opportunity to seek the guidance from the spirit of the Ancestors and the wisdom found in experience. In this world of genuine peace and calm, the United Element is exposed and devoid of secrets and hidden yearnings. The stars that litter the skies offer the palest of light, illuminating a sense of hope and encouragement, and the United Element discovers the truth found in trust, and armed with this knowledge, realises where it is heading in the greater scheme of things. It is from the depths of the Pool of Memories that the United Element's remembrances and dreams resurface for it to consider and ponder; a process that is typical of the Underworld. Some of the memories will be happy, while others will not, but the United Element will be expected to look closely at them all before being allowed to move on.

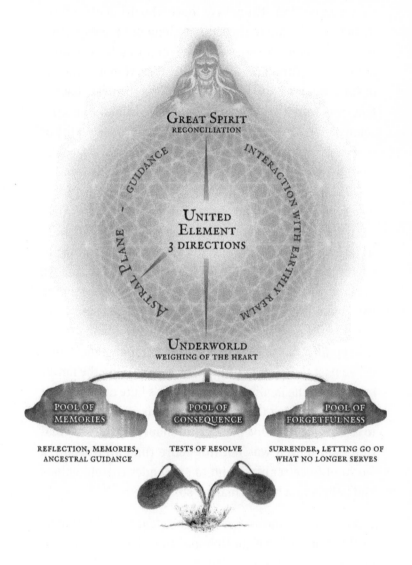

GREAT SPIRIT
RECONCILIATION

GUIDANCE

INTERACTION WITH EARTHLY REALM

ASTRAL PLANE

UNITED
ELEMENT
3 DIRECTIONS

UNDERWORLD
WEIGHING OF THE HEART

POOL OF
MEMORIES

POOL OF
CONSEQUENCE

POOL OF
FORGETFULNESS

REFLECTION, MEMORIES,
ANCESTRAL GUIDANCE

TESTS OF RESOLVE

SURRENDER, LETTING GO OF
WHAT NO LONGER SERVES

The third and final pool the United Element will deal with is the Pool of Forgetfulness; a pool where the water promises complete forgetfulness to those who drink or bathe in it. In truth, it's up to the United Element to decide what memories, once raised, should be forgotten or, as course of human nature, are intentionally forgotten as a means of survival. It's here, at the Pool of Forgetfulness that the fears and worries that unexpectedly rise from the subconscious mind are given the chance to manifest as reality or to withdraw again before being realised. It's where the United Element is given the choice to surrender the memories of the past and to move on, to receive the healing it deserves and to plan for a more positive life when it next incarnates. In life, some of us experience great difficulty in letting go because we're not aware of the chance to surrender negative or burdensome memories so that we may move on. It's a fine line indeed that separates 'living your lot in life' and dwelling on the past. Emotional pain never really heals. It's a like a river that flows and the key to keeping it flowing is to know how to remove the debris of the past that threatens to block it, hindering the newer energy and the healing it offers. So, it's here at the Pool of Forgetfulness that the United Element is given the chance to realise the life it lived was a life shaped by the imagination – a life that was nothing more than an illusion, a world of false reality – and to surrender the old values and beliefs that helped make it so.

Some may assume and, as a result, fear that the Underworld is no different to Hell and that the Devil himself must surely live there, and then to subsequently learn that the United Element consciously decides to venture into its depths may seem shocking. But for me the Underworld has nothing to do with the concept of Hell or the existence of the Devil as an external, malevolent being that loves nothing more than to torment and punish the spirits of those who find themselves in his domain. And even if the Devil did hold a place in the Underworld, it would only exist as a representation of the shadow aspect of our own self, the repressed, unmentioned, unspeakable desires we keep secret and locked away, or the personification of the turmoil, ignorance and despair that intermittently wracks our mind and body – that part of our mind that believes we are nothing without our worldly possessions, and that part of our self that repeatedly falls prey to the seductive pull of the material world, blinding us of our slavery to them.

During its stay in the Underworld which, like the time spent on the Earthbound Plane, may last up to seven generations in our world, the United Element frees itself of all trace of ego and the remnants of its familiar self and transforms into a pure expression of true bliss that's totally devoid of fear or worry. Having undergone a powerful rebirth of sorts, the United Element is both purified and rejuvenated and as such, no longer holds on to regret from the past or any other product of ignorance. Knowing the day may come when it may need to answer for some of the decisions it made while on the Earth Plane, it's at this point the United Element adjusts its future by deciding which values and beliefs to keep and which to let go.

It's also here in the Underworld that the United Element decides how it would like to be remembered to those still living, and what sort of legacy it wants to leave for not only its children (if it had children while alive) but also for humanity. We may assume we would have already determined this aspect of our journey before our death and to a large degree we have, especially in a physical sense. We may have worked hard during life, for example, accruing reputation, wealth, cars, boats and real estate, which we are able to bequeath to our family and friends. And we may die leaving our loved ones with good memories and loving thoughts, but unless we are prepared to let go of personal feelings of anger, resentment, jealousy and the countless other negative emotions that weigh the soul down during life, then the residual energy of those emotions will forever weigh heavily on the minds and hearts of those left behind after we die. The sooner the United Element can surrender any residual negative emotions harboured in life, the quicker this heaviness can lift for those still living, freeing them up to celebrate the legacy of love it deserves to inherit. It is only then, when the United Element finally attains peace in the knowing that its work and deeds will be remembered long after its death and after coming to terms with the knowledge that its earthly endeavours have had an impact on not just its family and friends but also the greater world and the Universe as well, that it can finally rest in the knowing it has truly lived life to the full, in every sense of the word.

Great Spirit

Simultaneously to the time it spends on the Earthbound Plane and in the Underworld, the final third of the United Element's journey sees it ascending to the Realm of Great Spirit, God or the Creator (or whoever the person prayed to in life) and, for want of a better description, plugs back into the essence of Creation to heal, replenish and sustain a person's spirit life force. Keeping in mind that this realm is not the Afterworld but rather a kind of annex or green room that mirrors the energy of the Afterworld without offering direct access to it, it is here that the United Element reconnects with the Creator. During its stay, the United Element is afforded opportunity to reconcile any ill feelings it may have fostered during life (particularly with its perception of God); feelings such as the false belief it was forsaken or somehow overlooked or forgotten, and anyone else it may have felt badly about when alive.

To provide the United Element with the chance to comprehend the karmic consequences of the decisions, actions and reactions it may have made during life, it is given sound opportunity to decide how the lessons hidden in those experiences may be learned or made peace with before it next incarnates.

It is also in this realm that I believe the presence of Angels, Ascended Teachers and Spirit Guides come into play, even if only on a vibrational level, and it is where the United element is required to spend time listening, taking in, absorbing, adapting to or consciously accepting the download of their wisdom so that it may learn how it may advance and grow in ways that will see it better serve the planet.

The Great Hall

Keeping in mind that the flow of time in a Pure Land (such as in Heaven and Shambhala) is totally different to time as we understand it, and a few days there equals many years here on Earth, it is therefore easy to comprehend how several generations could come and go for us while for the United Element, only a few years or even months may have transpired. So, by the time we have come to terms with the loss of our loved one, and perhaps several generations have passed and most of our soul family have united in the Underworld and have gone through their own transitional periods, the United Element will have completed its own journey and the three once autonomous aspects will have now merged to form a whole.

But instead of them coming together in any of the three realms it has just visited, this reunion takes place in a fourth and final leg of their journey and this location looks and feels like a massive hall or auditorium. While the soul and spirit are still melded as one (remembering that the soul cannot exist without the spirit), they are now able to interact independently of the other, which is important because it's here in the Great Hall that the United Elements (soul/spirits) of all our loved ones, family, distant relatives, friends, associates (formal and informal) and many others we've never met and never will, gather together and share stories of their journeys through the Astral Plane, Underworld and the Afterworld. They share what they've learned, how they've changed because of the experience, and the decisions and the pacts they've made with themselves and the Creator. More importantly, though, it's here that everyone sits down in their Soul Group and petitions one another to decide when they will reincarnate and how. For example, just because Joe was Mary's brother in their previous lives, doesn't mean they will reincarnate back into those same roles. If Mary had always mothered her little brother in life, then perhaps in their next incarnation Mary could decide to be Joe's mother and Joe may decide to come back as a female instead of a male. But assuming Joe hadn't lived a good and wholesome life, and had abused or harmed someone while he was Mary's brother, then he may decide that in the next life it will be time to deal with some of his karmic lessons and perhaps agree to experience abuse himself so that his soul may learn what it feels like and thereby knowing for eternity to never repeat that mistake again.

What may feel like a lifetime may be spent in the Great Hall and its grounds and surrounding districts which, when considered in its entirety, are more like a world than a building in a city somewhere. In fact, the kingdom in which the Great Hall exists reminds me a lot of the Wiccan Summerland; a perfect place for rest, recuperation and remembering. What's surprising about the Great Hall is that everyone in attendance is able to experience many of the same things they may have done in life, such as eating and drinking, shopping, attending parties, visiting the park, going to the movies and spending time with friends and family. Being that we no longer have a physical body, we no longer hold the need to experience things in a physical manner. The only difference remaining is that the notion of eating a meal becomes a sensory experience rather than a physical act, that is, smelling the aroma of a dish replaces the need to taste and digest it. What may once have needed to be touched to be understood, for example, must now be witnessed vibrationally or perceptually in the Great Hall. What may have once needed to be heard to be appreciated (like music, a bird's call or the sound of rain or waves crashing onto rocks), can now be experienced as emotions or feelings.

While everything remains the same as it was in life, nothing happens the same as it once did. It's in the Great Hall too, that we are expected to take what we learned while in the attendance of the Creator, under the supervision of the of Angels, Ascended Teachers and Spirit Guides, and to put theory into practice. For example, if Peter was a bit of a racist in life, he may be expected to spend time at a cultural centre or some other facility that offers authentic ethnic experiences and traditional teachings of ALL the cultures Peter had once demonstrated an intolerance toward. Another example might be that Steve only had time for 'the boys' while he was alive, and so rarely gave credence to the wants or needs of his wife – or women in general for that matter – and so while in the Great Hall he may be expected to experience the role of a woman and to dedicate himself to learning all about childbirth, parenthood, emotions, love, empathy, equality and what it means to not only be a lover, husband and father, but also a true man, friend, partner, role model and confidant.

Veronica may have lived her life as a corporate woman, dedicating herself to the attainment of wealth, status and social standing, and as part of her re-education she may be expected to experience the consequences of extreme poverty, homelessness, isolation, social division and even mental health.

In life, Arthur and his wife Patricia may have both been people of science, who exhibited little patience for musicians, artists, dreamers or anyone that exhibited a bohemian or spiritual outlook on life. But, in the Great Hall, both Arthur and Patricia may be required to spend time delving into the more free-thinking, intuitive, creative and less logical ways of exploring life as part of their experience.

But before Peter, Steve, Veronica, Arthur, Patricia or anyone else who finds themselves in the Great Hall can be expected to know where to start, how to adjust to this new extraordinary yet non-ordinary way of living, or to understand what they need to do to honour the wishes of the Angels, Ascended Teachers and Spirit Guides, there is an orientation process that they must first take part in so that everything flows the way it is meant to.

The Master Guide

The first being the newly arrived United Element meets when landing in the Great Hall is its Master Guide, who is immediately recognised as the most sacrosanct of all guides. The Master Guide is different to the Spirit Guides who, along with the Ascended Teachers and Angels, exist alongside the Creator on a higher plane or higher vibrational stage of existence. Our Spirit Guides, the Ascended Teachers and Angels aren't likely to manifest in the Great Hall but can be accessed through our Master Guide who acts like a messenger or channel and a filter of sorts by 'dumbing down' the wisdom being imparted so the United Element can comprehend what they're wanting to say. With the support of the Master Guide, the Spirit Guides, Ascended Teachers and Angels can offer the United Element higher teachings and deeper wisdom during and between their earthly incarnations.

Everyone who arrives in the foyer of the Great Hall for the first time is allocated a Master Guide. While it cannot be guaranteed, the Master Guide may be someone the United Element knew personally or knew of during their last life. The Master Guide is a chaperon of sorts, designated solely to one United Element, and it's this chaperon's role to show it around the Great Hall, its grounds and surrounding districts, and to explain how things happen, why and when. The Master Guide's role is to also move the United Element into their new 'house', introducing it to its new 'neighbours' and reuniting it with those it knew in life. They also spend time enquiring about the interests, hobbies and special abilities the United Element participated in while on Earth, and what its belief systems, values, likes and fears centred on. The role of the Master Guide extends beyond the United Element's time in the Great Hall though, spilling into its next incarnation and staying with it for the duration of its next earthly existence.

While others may disagree, I believe the Master Guide's role is reassessed after each entire rotation through life and after death, and it's not until the United Element once again finds itself in the Great Hall that it is decided by the Angels and Ascended Teachers if a new Master Guide needs to be allocated or whether the same one will be retained. While in the Great Hall though, it is the role of the Master Guide to explain the process of reincarnation, the notion of karma and how to evolve and eventually be welcomed into the Afterworld and permitted to stay, and what the United Element must do to ensure all goes to plan. Over time, the input of the Master Guide becomes less and less obvious to the United Element, meaning their need to consciously step in will lessen over time, to the point where it will be hardly noticed at all. But no matter how long the United Element remains in the Great Hall, the Master Guide will be there at their side, with no thought of moving on or taking on another dependant. The United Element is never alone, even after it reincarnates on the Astral Plane. It never feels lonely and will never be expected to assume or figure things out for itself while it remains a resident of the Great Hall.

The Healers

The experiences the United Element had while in the land of the living influences what counselling it will require after death, and whether it will need to spend time with one or more of the Healers that work at the Great Hall. On advice from the Master Guide, the United Element may find itself in what could be described as a hospital or healing room for any length of time. The purpose of the Healers is to help the United Element recover from the residual effects of a severe illness leading up to and resulting in its death, or the injuries sustained because of a car, boat, train, aeroplane or some other accident that saw it pass from our world into the land of the dead.

Trauma experienced by the physical body before death, albeit a result of addiction or some other form of self-abuse, illness, surgery or an accident of any kind, needs to be given time to heal properly after death to allow the United Element the chance to fully restore and replenish its vitality.

It is also the role of the Healer to double as a therapist of sorts, to help the United Element recover from shock, fear or emotional trauma it may have faced leading up to its death. In the case of murder victims and souls that took their own lives, either intentionally by means of suicide or inadvertently because of alcohol or substance abuse, reckless behaviour or misadventure, the Healer's primary role is to support the United Element as a counsellor, as it deals with and goes through the five stages of grief: denial, anger, bargaining, depression and acceptance. You would think those left behind would be the only ones dealing with grief after losing a loved one, but that's not the case. Even the dead go through stages of grief, and they experience all the emotions that we feel as they fight to come to terms with their own demise. It's true that we, as the living, feel deeply robbed when someone dies of natural causes, let alone unnatural ones and often requiring counselling to help us deal with the reality and permanence of death. No matter how much warning we are given leading up to someone's passing, the arrival of the final breath always comes as a shock. But the horror we feel when someone we love is taken from us unexpectedly or under shocking conditions can prove to be too much for some people, crippling the mind and spirit, with the burden of both physically overwhelming them, rendering them incapable of living a productive life. So, you can imagine the United Element – the soul and spirit of those we love – walking with us on the Astral Plane during its Earthbound phase of existence, witnessing its still-living family and friends coming to terms with its death and seeing them break down and often struggle to find the will to get back up. All this trauma is borne equally by the dead, with the guilt they feel for putting us through the pain matching the suffering we feel in losing them. Hence the necessity for and unquestionable importance of the Healers, who are fully equipped to support those we've lost and to help them surrender any feelings of responsibility.

Sometimes those left behind harbour a fear that if someone ends their own life, they will somehow be punished for their actions when they arrive in the Afterworld. But, because there is nothing in the Christian Bible that forbids or condemns suicide, this is an unfounded fear for Christians in particular. It has probably been fuelled by the misinformed, the teachings of other faiths, or those who see it as their right to speak on behalf of the Creator. In fact, the Bible shares accounts of people that have committed suicide, so even though the Roman Catholic Church may argue that suicide violates the commandment 'thou shalt not kill', the severity of the consequence and the level of 'blame' dramatically changes due to the nature of the circumstances. Besides, the Bible states that God is happy to forgive (the grief it may have caused those still living), so long as the person shows remorse for their decision, while the Church openly offers prayers for those who have taken their own life, which is something they wouldn't do if suicide was a sin. So, it is the role of the Healers to reassure the United Element that it will not be punished for its decision to end its own life, and to help it find peace in that knowledge.

It is also the role of the Healers to help the United Element realise that, if it lived a selfish or greedy life or if it some-how treated others badly in mind or deed, or even if it ignored its commitments or turned its back on responsi-bilities to pursue other interests or lifestyle, this may affect its chances of moving forward unless it shows accountability for its choices. This realisation sometimes comes as a terrible surprise followed by feelings of shame and sorrow because even after death, the deceased simply fail to recognise or understand the error of their ways. So, it is the role of the Healer to once again don their counsel-lor hat as they support the United Element through the process of acceptance and answerability, after which the mantle is passed on to other members of the crew stationed within the walls of the Great Hall.

The Coaches

Oftentimes, after the United Element spends time in the care of the Healer, it must then employ the services of a Coach whose role it is to walk it through the process of putting things right. It's all very well for the United Element to be shown how it messed up in certain areas of life, but there's no point in expecting it to know how to fix its mistakes or create peace in the lives of those directly affected by its decisions and actions without some sort of guidance or help. So, with the support of the Coach, the United Element must review once again its life, and pay witness to the after-effects of its behaviour while alive. If, for example, 'Sidney' was a married man who had affairs and kept mistresses and effectively lived a double life that didn't include his wife, and after seeing for himself the pain and suffering his infidelity infringed on the mental and emotional wellbeing of his spouse, the Coach may instruct the United Element to help a living soul find true love by guiding her hand into that of a more loving, respectful and deserving man.

Perhaps 'Angela' was a chronic gambler who squandered her wages in the casino, leaving her family destitute, hungry and unable to afford warm clothes. The role of the Coach here may be to inspire someone affected by poverty to tap into their own gifts and awaken their entrepreneurial spirit, to shape their own destiny and build their own wealth without the need to rely on anyone else.

The role of the Coach is to help the United Element put things right by turning its own faults and weaknesses into Gifts of Power. Those in the land of the living may feel as though their luck has inexplicably changed, or that their Guardian Angel had, for some reason, decided to shine its light on their life and to spin the Wheel of Destiny in their favour. And in many ways, they would be right.

The Pearly Gates

While others may believe we go straight to the Afterworld after we die, I tend not to. Well, not the first time around at least. It's my opinion that we journey through many lives incarnating countless times, with the sole purpose of improving and perfecting ourselves, while building a reservoir of good karma along the way.

It's not until we totally understand and appreciate every aspect and emotion of bodily human reality, and when we've reached spiritual purity after surrendering ego and all negative sentiment, when we've attained true peace in the knowing that our earthly endeavours have favourably impacted our family and friends, the greater world and the Universe for which we will be remembered and celebrated long after our death, that we are then finally able to approach the vestibule affectionately known as the Pearly Gates, and then enter the Afterworld.

The Afterworld is the final station of our soul's greater journey because it is in the Afterworld that we are welcome to stay for eternity, to live a golden life in a pure world devoid of shadows, reasoning and attainable knowledge, as well as the seven capital vices that include pride, greed, lust, envy, gluttony, wrath and sloth, sent to test the living at every turn. As a final threshold, the Pearly Gates are truly the ultimate destination. If going on an expedition in search of moral or spiritual consequence, even if only a metaphorical quest in search of our own beliefs or to understand our own mortality, then the journey of the spirit to the Afterworld is by far the supreme pilgrimage.

Satori, enlightenment and death of the ego self

According to Zen Buddhism, there is a state of enlightenment a student may attain after much study and dedica-
tion through deep meditation known as 'satori'. From the
Japanese satoru, satori is a term that equates to awakening, comprehension and understanding. As an experience,
however, satori refers to the process of 'seeing into one's
own true nature' or essence. To attain true enlightenment,
the student must first acquire a pure perception of both
the nature-self, or emptiness (kenshō), as well as a heightened level of awareness regarding their interaction with
life and the world (satori). While some believe kenshō and
satori are the same thing, the attainment of enlightenment can include both.

Similarly, directly after death, after the deceased's soul
(ba) is reduced to a blueprint and merges, as a lesser off-
shoot, with the deceased's spirit (ka) to create a new element (akh). But before this new element cohesively 'splits'
to become the United Element and continue to simultaneously but independently explore the Astral Plane, the
Underworld and the Realm of the Great Spirit, it may first
experience a miraculous realisation – satori or a state of
pure and lasting enlightenment. It is at this point, soon
after death, that the deceased's ego dies and, like the Zen
Buddhist student, he or she is said to not only experience
unadulterated emptiness, but to also hopefully catch a
glimpse of their true essence, or rather the pure realisation of who he or she was; their true self, who they were in
life, why they were like that and how they came to be that
person. And it is at this point, during this sacred moment
when life becomes death and when the physical has

reached a crux, that it is hoped the deceased attains true enlightenment. I say 'hoped' because, if the truth be told, a person may live and die countless times, transmigrating from one soul experience to another as they search to realise their life path which will see them living their true life's purpose and realising the work of Great Spirit. Until that time comes though, they will continue to take the cyclical journey in a bid to realise true satori.

Reaching a state of satori even after death is not something that just happens. It must be attained, and for many, attainment may take lifetimes to secure. But regardless how long it takes, the cycle must be repeated again and again until satori has been reached because it's only when it is attained that the United Element can realise what level of awareness is required to be formally welcomed and allowed access to and permitted to remain in the Afterworld.

Past Lives and Reincarnation

There are countless stories published in books, available online or retold in television documentaries, of children as young as two making announcements of 'being someone else' in another time, or once 'belonging to a different family'. I remember reading an account that told of an Australian couple who, when approaching a small English country town while on holiday, were surprised to hear their small child say, 'I used to live here', before describing in detail his old school, the church he attended every Sunday and the house he used to inhabit with his 'other parents'. They were shocked as they then passed the establishments described by their son, all of which matched his descriptions precisely. While adults sometimes experience spontaneous flashbacks or recollections of past lives perhaps while meditating or dreaming, under hypnosis or during facilitated past life regressions, it seems to be that children are either more receptive (in that their minds are still clear of a lot of the indoctrinated beliefs about what's possible and what's not) or we're all offered temporary windows of opportunity to remember being here before that gradually fades.

As I mentioned earlier, it is my opinion that we journey through many lives, incarnating countless times, with the sole purpose of improving and perfecting ourselves while accruing a bank of good karmic points along the way. What we 'get wrong' in one life can be revisited, reviewed and repaired during the next if we so choose. It's not that we are offered a choice of if we *want* to face our life lessons, but rather *when*. No matter what, we must face them and the longer we delay the process, the more times we will need to incarnate before we are deemed ready to journey to the Afterworld. If Grace lived her life as a thief in this life, for example, she may be forced to endure being regularly stolen from in the next. While Ruben may have taken mistresses in this life, only to have someone covet and purloin the love of his life, breaking his heart beyond repair during a future incarnation. The golden rule worth remembering when contemplating reincarnation is: 'What goes around, comes around.' Another rule could be 'an eye for an eye', with what you ignore, take advantage of or abuse in this life guaranteed to be recompensed in kind three-fold in the next.

Sometimes, friendships, associations and romantic relationships that we have forged in this lifetime have roots or origins established in previous lifetimes and not necessarily in our most recent one. Also, the way these friendships, associations and relationships pan out often have reasons set in motion in those previous incarnations. For example, I believe the bond I shared with my two friends that died in a car accident was birthed in a previous life. I don't know if we had been blood brothers or not, but I had a dream once where the three of us shared a cell in an institution of some sort. The youngest brother was the eldest of the two in this previous life, and he had blonde curly hair unlike the dark hair he sported in this life. The institution was solid brick, very cold with high-set windows and long, winding hallways, much like a 19th-century orphanage or similar. I was also shown a woman that used to come and look after us and who would bring food and water. Then one day she came for me and I was taken away. I promised the boys I'd come back for them someday and for whatever reason, I never got the opportunity. The strange thing is, after waking from that dream I knew the guy who was driving the car the night of the accident was, in this past life recollection, the woman who brought us food...

Despite this very vivid dream, I've often sat and pondered the validity of the notion of past lives. I've seriously asked myself if I am truly able to accept the experiences many of us claim to remember as past lives, or if we are in fact confusing them with things our Ancestors may have witnessed during a lifetime before we were born. While I am not denying the occurrence of past lives, I can't help but wonder that what many of us are assuming are past life memories may perhaps be the result of cellular memory activation.

The transmigration of the soul

Similar to, but different from, the notion of reincarnation where the United Element is reborn into a new body with each lifetime it enters, is a process known as *transmigration* or metempsychosis whereby the spirit is reborn into other sentient but typically non-human forms, such as: animals, birds, insects and fish; inanimate-yet-still-living objects such as stones, crystals; life forms such as trees, plants and herbs; or other expressions of life such as mountains and rivers. Unlike reincarnation, the process of transmigration sees the spirit not needing to be renewed or burdened by the soul of its previous existence, but rather, transferred to a new body with a new soul and a new consciousness, so that it may relive its previous earthly existence in order to relearn the same karmic lessons before even considering going any further on its spiritual journey.

For Indigenous Australian people, the Dreamtime was the time before time, when the world was new, and the Ancestor Spirits still wandered on Earth (often in human shape, sometimes not), helping to bring form to the land, the plants and the animals. It was when everything on the horizon was being created and when everything was getting used to being. Some Indigenous Australians refer to this time as The Dreamtime, while others refer to their personal spiritual connection to the Ancients and the land as The Dreaming. As the Ancestor Spirits roamed on Earth, they set about forming links between groups and individuals, some of which were human while some were not. As they travelled, they fashioned the ground by creating mountains and valleys, rivers and streams. Places marked by the Ancestors held great spiritual significance to the people, with stories and legends related to their Dreaming emerging as a way of explaining this sacred time of Creation. After the Ancestors had finished influencing the land, some returned to the stars or the earth itself, while others transmigrated to become people or other things such as animals, birds, mountains and streams. This was a sacred time, alive with the magic of Creation; a time now gone, but still imbued with great power for the people who continue to believe that the Ancestor Spirits are still here, disguised in the forms they took when Earth was new.

Whereas some Indigenous Australian people continue to believe, with details varying from one nation or language group to the next, that infants can be born as reincarnations of Ancestral Spirits, with the soul being everlasting and continuously moving from one generation to the next, some Indonesian groups believe that the human soul can transmigrate into the bodies of animals considered to be spiritually sacred, even if only temporarily, as if preparing for their next human incarnation. Similarly, several west Amazonian and even some African tribal groups avoid eating certain animals because they believe these animals house significant Ancestral Spirits, thus marking them as sacred.

Cellular memory

Not to be confused with genetic memory, which is memory that is present the moment we are born without the benefit of sensory experience, cellular memory is knowledge that is genetically ingrained; for example, how to do things without ever needing to be shown, taught or told, such as our inherent capacity to recognise our parents and the innate ability to learn language. My father-in-law used to point with his middle finger when drawing someone's attention to something in the distance and without ever meeting his grandfather or being told of this habit, my youngest son – from a very young age – has always favoured pointing with his middle finger. Cellular memory, as I explain in my book *Earth Mother Dreaming*, is something we all carry and it's something we're all able to access whenever we choose.

Every cell in the human body is a living, conscious entity, willingly working together for the good of the whole. In truth, the wellbeing of the individual is secondary. If necessary, the cells will die to protect the body and they often do. The lifetime of a cell lasts but an instant when compared to that of a human. We lose thousands of skin cells every hour; immune cells sacrifice themselves to fight off incoming bacteria and germs. Self-interest is never the agenda. Our cells evolve from one moment to the next. They're always in a state of flux, adapting and changing. They must be malleable so that they're able to handle whatever situation they're faced with. Being fixed prevents change and being unprepared to accept change leads to collapse and ill health. Our body 'knows' what we need to remember and through our sacred breath, we give it life.

Through every cell, through our very DNA, we hold memory of all things that have ever happened since the beginning of time. In fact, we hold all memory of the time before time – a time of 'timeless being' – The Dreaming: a time of recognition and great discovery, when all things were being created, when everything was deciding what was to be and when everything was 'learning' to exist. Memory of The Dreaming reminds us that we are capable of communing with the forces of Nature and to speak readily to the animals, birds, reptiles, fish and insects and Nature as a whole. In the World of Spirit, neither time nor life are linear. Nor do they rotate like a wheel or circle. Instead, they ebb and flow like an all-encompassing sphere, very much like Earth itself. Every grain of sand and every lump of dirt acts as living keys to the cache of memories stored deep within the Earth Mother's belly. And we do too, as the children of the Earth Mother. It's on this cellular degree that we all carry the experiences of our Ancestors, all those who have walked before us. We remember right back to the ignition of the first spark, the One Fire that represented the beginning of all life on Earth Mother. Our cellular memory acts as an unbroken thread of life that links us back to The Dreaming and the beginning of all things.

So, what if some of the experiences we assume are past life recollections are in fact experiences had by our Ancestors that are stored in our DNA? The main reason I question the soundness of many past life stories is that, in most cases, the individuals people believe they once were, are usually notable, high ranking or spiritually sound and are nearly always identified from a third-person perspective. For example, it's not uncommon for people who are recalling memories to make observations or to describe 'themselves' as if looking at themselves through the eyes of a bystander. If, for example, we truly were Cleopatra in a past life, and we were reliving that life either through meditation or via regression therapy, wouldn't we be seeing life through her eyes, looking at the world as she would have seen it? Surely, the ability to see yourself as the beautiful Egyptian Queen would not allow for clear vision of her makeup, the colour of her eyes or how perfect her nose and teeth were? Surely, our vision would be limited to those standing in front of us, or those washing our feet or approaching us from another room? Surely, if we were seeing Cleopatra as she sat perched on her golden, lapis-lazuli encrusted throne, then we might assume we weren't Cleopatra but rather the poor wretch at her feet as he nervously looks up at her for approval or further instruction? Food for thought.

But what if the memories we are recalling are in fact memories, but just not OUR memories? What if, for example, an officer of the Roman army in 30 BC during the defeat of Mark Antony and unseating of Queen Cleopatra by Octavian, played a major role in the takeover of Egypt and helped establish the Roman Empire's hold in the region? What if that same officer was then given extra privileges that saw him get to know Cleopatra before her untimely, self-induced death on 12 August 30 BC? What if the experience was so life-changing for the officer that he never forgot the beautiful Queen, and her memory was imprinted in his mind forever? And then that officer lived a good life under the protection of the Roman Empire before dying at a ripe old age on Egyptian soil? And what if many, many generations later, the descendants of that same officer now bear your family name and you discover that he was in fact one of your Ancestors? Perhaps, and it's just a thought, it was his memories you were recalling and not your own as you'd first assumed, held intact within your DNA. What if you were remembering his memories rooted in actual events thousands of years before you were even conceived? An interesting notion, huh?

Spirit Family and Soul Groups

I've often wondered why it is that we can walk past hundreds of people in a single day and never acknowledge any of them, let alone have a chat. And then, for some strange reason, one random day we may be sitting on a park bench and start chatting to a lady who's feeding the pigeons and, voila! a lifelong friendship ignites without anyone even trying! What makes that lady different to the people we happily pass in the street? What makes her so special? You may never have met this lady before but there's an inherent, gut feeling that you were supposed to meet because you share similar character traits, interests or, weirdly, mutual friends. There's something very familiar about her, to the point that she lives on the same street as you despite meeting in a park in another state to where you live! While this scenario may sound far-fetched, you'd be surprised how often this sort of 'chance meeting' happens.

I like to believe that when you meet and deeply connect with someone you've never met before, it's because you've known them from another time. If not this lifetime, perhaps a previous lifetime or from a lifetime so far back that their memory, though not available to you consciously, is deeply ingrained on a cellular level within your very makeup. It may be that this person was a friend or a lover, a family member or some other significant person in your life back then. Perhaps there are karmic lessons that are still needing to be learned, karmic favours that need to be repaid or karmic injustices that need to be put right, and if any of these are relevant to your present-day, reinstated relationship, then the Wheel of Fate will decide when and how these issues are to be addressed and resolved.

But sometimes these people come back into our life for no other reason than to reconnect and pick up from where they left off. Sometimes the only force at work is love, and if that's the case then you should consider yourself truly blessed to have found one another again. People that we reconnect with because of a one-time relationship founded in love, I believe, are members of our Spirit Family; a family forged from mutual respect, love, admiration and promise. I believe my wife was guided to me because she forms the hub of my Spirit Family. Sure, we are married with children in this lifetime, but we believe, in fact, we KNOW that we've been together in previous lifetimes and that we were guided back together to continue our journey this time around. And for no other reason but to celebrate love. It's a truth we both feel very deeply and it's a knowing we've never had reason to doubt or question.

I also have several friends that are so precious to me that I know our bond extends way beyond the boundaries of this life. The only way I can describe the relationship I share with these people is to celebrate them as my brothers and sisters, and when you can do this without question you know you're onto something, especially when you can say, 'I love you' to their faces and they believe you and respond in kind without feeling awkward, embarrassed or inappropriate. These people know who they are and when they read this, will know without having to ask whether I'm referencing them and the kinship we share, despite not being blood-related.

However, there are other people we meet along the Good Red Road of Life who, although they also hold an important place in our heart and are in our life without conflict or question for what may seem like forever with no thought of moving on or breaking away, will never feel as significant as those we deem to be Spirit Family. But these people are no less important to our life journey and while they may serve a different emotional purpose, they can be classified as members of our Soul Group. Those who belong to our Soul Group may share similar likes and dislikes, they may laugh at the same jokes we laugh at and enjoy the same food, holiday destinations and musical preferences, but they'll always just be dear friends. Those who belong to our Soul Group are people who may help us resolve karmic debts and so forth, or who we are drawn to support us as they repay theirs.

Soul Group members may come and go and even if you lose touch with them they will haunt your consciousness for the rest of your life. For example, you may find yourself thinking of them even if you have no desire or way to reach out to them and, while you are thinking of them, you can't help but wonder if they ever think of you. Those who belong to our Soul Group are people who have helped make us who we are today, be it in a good and loving way or not. They are people who you feel thankful for knowing, even if you have difficulty feeling grateful for the lessons you've had to learn from them.

Spirit Family, though, are people we love and know on a deeply. Sure, they can be considered friends or 'best' friends, but when you're with them you feel a bond that runs so deeply, you know your heart would surely break if it were to end. I think the only thing that blurs the line between what makes a person a member of your Soul Group or your Spirit Family in this life is that in both instances, the person can be blood-related. You can love your family, for example, but you don't have to like them. Similarly, you can like someone, and you can even go as far as to say you respect them, but you may never feel drawn to say you love them. Either way, some people feel as though they're in your life for reasons you cannot fully understand and it's these people that I truly believe you must have symbolically signed a spiritual contract with in a previous life or something similar, because if you were to be totally honest with yourself – why else would they be in your life?

Karma, Dharma and Fate

Spiritual contracts

No one can say for sure why it is that certain people become significant beings in our life, especially when the circumstances that bring them to us are random and the time they spend with us is brief. Some people are just not meant to be with us in this life forever. At first glance, these people seem to come into our life to stir things up or make things happen. Sometimes they bring happiness and sometimes they bring grief. They may start off as friends of friends or work associates, and then over time become important to us. And then one day, often for reasons we cannot explain, the friendship falls apart and we part ways. But as if by design, they always leave a legacy that either makes us glad to have had the privilege of calling them friends or leaves us wishing we'd never laid eyes on them. The fact that we did lay eyes on them, however, was not by chance. It was meant to be, set up before we were born, perhaps during our time spent in the Great Hall prior to our incarnation into this life.

While I don't believe we can set a date and time to meet these people as we sit in the Great Hall, I believe there's some degree of free will that's allowed to play out. And meet them we will, without a doubt. There's no chance of missing them or not being in the right place at the right time because it has been preordained that the meeting will occur and that we will connect. It's just a matter of when, where and how. And the reason it's so definite is because we signed a contract with them before we were born that mutually binds us to the fact. We cannot avoid it, nor can we change our mind and break the contract because, like all contracts, when you sign, it's locked in stone.

It's hard to imagine that we sign what's called a spiritual contract before entering the Earth Plane, but we do. The purpose of the spiritual contract is to ensure we stick to our side of the deal, and that we don't forget, change our mind or play dumb and deny ever making the pact. We sign spiritual contracts for all number of reasons, usually with people who have nominated themselves (or who have been nominated by a third party) to bring about change that will see us grow, heal and lead the life we were destined to live.

For example, I believe there was a spiritual contract in place between me and the friends that died in the car accident. I believe that, at some point it was arranged that their time on this beautiful blue and green planet would be cut short, and that their passing would trigger a memory deep within me reminding me of my greater purpose. Up until they died, I was happy – but not content – and living a mainstream, average life. I knew the day would come where I would be forced to deal with my childhood, but it never occurred to me that my life held greater purpose, or that my childhood abuse would provide me with such a deep sense of compassion for my fellow humans, let alone awaken within me the profound spiritual connection to the Animal Realm that I'm now known for. Who would have thought that such a tragic event could lead to the realisation of greater purpose? To be honest, I felt I had no choice but to do what I could to honour their death by making it mean something. The very thought that they'd lived and died for no reason made me sick with grief, so the only right thing to do was to turn the darkness of despair that haunted my soul into a light that I could follow and ultimately become.

Spiritual contracts often manifest in ways we would never have chosen ourselves. For example, after a minor altercation Allen's long-time friend suddenly turns against him and decides to sue him for money his friend believes he is owed. Allen is summonsed to court, and after losing the case finds himself legally bound to repay his friend but is also forced to declare bankruptcy. Allen could easily decide to seek revenge against his one-time friend, but he realises the issue goes way beyond this lifetime and decides instead to thank him and ponder the greater purpose of this chapter of his life. In doing so, Allen honours the spiritual contract he signed with his friend prior to his present life and, after learning the lesson, turns his near financial ruin into something wonderful and dies a wealthy and successful businessman.

Library of Records

Within the grounds of the Great Hall is a space known as the Library of Records. In truth, it's more like another great hall but it's easier to conceptualise when described as a library. The rooms within the library, have high vaulted ceilings and they are full of floor-to-ceiling shelves stacked with boxes (for want of a better description) containing the files of every single human being that has ever existed. The files list all the experiences every living being has had, including every hope, wish and desire, event, thought, word, emotion and intent, as well as by whom, when and where they took place, and why. And it's here, in the Library of Records, that every karmic debt yet to be repaid, every karmic lesson yet to be learned, every karmic favour yet be returned and every karmic injustice yet to be remedied are documented, stored and time-lined for acknowledgement and settlement, along with the names of all parties involved and the facts surrounding the case – be they assumed, imagined, fabricated or real, along with the outcome and how the case has been or is yet to be reconciled.

Every situation and circumstance – past, present or future – is listed in the Library of Records and this is how it has always been and how it will always be. Also in the Library of Records is the Book of Life, which lists the name of every soul that's ever incarnated on the planet, along with every good deed they've ever done which, when reviewed and added up as points after they've passed from the

Earth Plane, accrues as good karma; just the thing you need when serious about entering the Afterworld.

The Records, including the entries in the *Book of Life*, are made energetically and not by some dedicated team of spirits who are employed to watch everything we do. If we could imagine that the Records look like a long roll of parchment and that whenever anything significant happens in our life, it is automatically recorded on this parchment down to the last detail and appears magically like a message written in lemon juice will do when gently heated. All our actions and reactions, responses, thoughts and deeds are transliterated by invisible hands, in real time, the moment they happen.

Some people believe the Records are chronicled in a system not that dissimilar to the way newspapers and other public documents were stored on microfiche files. Some people believe our Guardian Angels do the recording, while others believe it is God himself who makes note of everything we think and do. Personally, I believe a being as mighty as God, let alone his Angels, would most certainly have better things to do to keep their days full than sit, watch and report on the comings and goings of every single human being on the planet on any given day. Therefore, the recording of those sacred files needs to be super-efficient, hence the notion of them being recorded energetically, as if caught on surveillance camera and transcribed into text by some highly efficient, unearthly computer.

The Library of Records is self-governing, meaning that it is operates under its own volition. This happens so there can be no confusion of the facts or interference or molestation by any external force. So much so that, unlike other libraries, there are no attendees or library staff to monitor the logged files because there is simply no need. No one can borrow the files, and no one manually adds to the 'collection'. There are no incomings or outgoings. The files are closed, sitting there silently, being energetically added to every second of every day.

But when the day comes for an individual's file to be opened for their life events and karma to be reviewed, the recording stops and everything about them is opened for analysis by their Master Guide, the Council of Elders and, perhaps if required and depending on the case and how the spirit (the United Element) lived life, an ambassador chosen to speak on behalf of the Angelic realms and the Creator. In similar fashion to the weighing of the heart, everyone in attendance sits with the spirit at a table with no leader, and collectively decides what forms of remuneration or compensation the spirit needs to pay back, to whom, in what form and for what reason, and then in turn, what reward or recompense is owed to the spirit by other parties, as well as how it is to be repaid and to what extent it is deserving.

Universal Law

It is Universal Law that states everyone must have their records analysed before they can be allowed to reincarnate. Everyone must have their karmic 'bank account' reviewed, and everyone must be held accountable for their actions and reactions during life. No one can avoid this process and when our time comes, we will be expected to acknowledge the consequences of our deeds, both good and bad, and to take responsibility for the ripple effects of those choices.

And it is Universal Law that states every action triggers a reaction. Known as the Butterfly Effect, there is a theory that explains that when a small change takes place within an initial set of circumstances, big changes – that may not become evident until much later – can be triggered. These changes often begin as a small ripple, caused by a pebble being thrown into a rockpool at some undefined time or place, but when left to their own devices without interference, may be experienced much later as a tsunami hitting a distant shore. Like when a squirrel buries an acorn with the intention of digging it up later, if forgotten and left to germinate and grow, the acorn later becomes a tree capable of sustaining not just the squirrel, but also its future generations.

It is also Universal Law that every single soul that incarnates has the right to free will (meaning that they are encouraged to decide what's right for them and what's not) and to live according to those decisions in any way they see fit. Sure, there are other laws stating that when a soul incarnates they must do what they can to never bring harm to any other living being, be it intentional or not, and that to live outside this simple rule will bring consequences that often outweigh the misdeed. But the truth of the matter is, how we act will ultimately trigger reactions that may not be felt until after our death, and if not then, when we reincarnate next time round.

Unlike the legal system we have here on Earth, Universal Law is governed by love. No matter how life may unfold for us as human beings, the foundation of our path through life is, and always will be, paved by love. Before we entered this plane, every cobblestone used to build the road we choose to walk during life was forged from love and, no matter how much we may argue, there is no escaping the fact that every single one of us was birthed into this world with nothing but love in our hearts. The circumstances we found ourselves in when we 'landed' may have been anything but loving, and the experiences we faced as we walked through life may have done everything in their power to crush any trace of love we were born with out of every cell in our being, but when we decided to reincarnate, our heart was brimming with Universal Love. Love is all there is, and that's Universal Law. And it is up to us if we choose to remember this simple fact as we journey the Good Red Road of Life. It is up to us as human beings to decide how we live our life. Of all the planes of existence our soul and spirit will encounter, the Earth Plane is the densest. Wrought with physical experiences, challenges and pain, life is pitted with countless degrees of emotion, grief, loss, physical hurt, suffering, torment and confusion. But it is also important to remember that it is also rich with unlimited love and opportunity.

As human beings living in a world that is now largely ruled by materialism, fear and greed, we find ourselves focusing more on the negative, even though love and beauty still exist in abundance, all around us, every second of every day. We've unconsciously allowed the darkness of pain, confusion and anger to invade our heart and minds, and over time we, as a race, have forsaken love and beauty. Some of us succumb to the darkness so much that we become the darkness, and the path of love that we were born to live is left far behind never to be walked again. Most of us, however, yearn to return to love and beauty but we have no idea where to find it, let alone what it looks and feels like. We go through life assuming love has forsaken us, so much so that even if it slapped us in the face we wouldn't notice it being there, standing right in front of us with its nose pressed firmly against ours.

Love is the joy I feel when my kids call me Dad. It is the unquestionable devotion I feel for my wife and the commitment she feels for me. It is the miracle of watching a duckling hatch from an egg or the flowers blooming in the garden. It is the crack of thunder, the changing of the seasons, the morning sun, the purr of a cat and the sound of rain on the roof. It is laughter, tears and memories from long ago. It is the knowing that I have friends who would do anything for me, and the surprise seen on their face when I do something unexpected for no other reason but to see that look. Love is these things. It is the beauty that surrounds us all, and when I think of it, I am humbled beyond compare. I am literally brought to tears because it is such a big and mighty force that exists solely for us. A force so powerful that it can only be found in the simplest, smallest and subtlest of things. Love is always there, in plain view. It doesn't avoid us or shy away when we reach out to it. It is freely and willingly available to all of us. But it is our perception of the world and our choice, and ours alone, that determines whether we acknowledge and embrace it or to turn our back on it and walk away.

Love is all there is, be it in this life and the next and every life thereafter. This is Universal Law. Even if we cannot remember what love looks or feels like, by simply acknowledging its existence (even if we're not sure that it does exist) and making a pact to do our best to welcome it into our life, things will start to change. The key is remaining vigilant for the signs and offering gratitude when we notice them. The more we show gratitude, the more love will flow into our life. And while all this might sound lovely, the crucial thing to truly hold close to our heart is that by welcoming love into our life and showing gratitude when we notice its presence, compassion, empathy, patience, tolerance and respect will gradually begin to replace feelings of resentment, anger, frustration, confusion and self-centredness. These new feelings will feel light, bringing with them thoughts of possibility and hope and a sense of balance. The more these feelings are nurtured and welcomed, too, the more we'll notice our life change for the better. It may take time and the process may be slow going, but the change will most definitely happen.

But that's not all. The more we focus on improving our attitude and perceptions in this life and the more we allow the love and beauty that surrounds us to infiltrate our being, our relationships and circumstances will also improve. We will eventually return to a state of love, even if we don't mean to. By opening ourselves to the notion of returning to a state of love, the intention alone will trigger a ripple effect that will see us restore our karmic credit. With every step we take toward living a good, positive and wholesome life, and the more we surrender to the process of returning to a state of love, the more our personal file in the Library of Records will be dotted with the Creator's version of those little golden star-shaped stickers we may have received as children for a job well done. And then when we eventually find ourselves in the Great Hall, our time there will be one filled with peace and beauty, ensuring a life filled with love next time around.

Spirit Children

Children of all ages pass away for a multitude of reasons but on a global scale, the five leading causes of death of a child under five years of age are pneumonia, premature birth, diarrhea, malaria and undernutrition. Other causes include stillbirth, Sudden Infant Death Syndrome (SIDS), accidents, poisoning and violence which, in my opinion, includes abuse of any kind and neglect.

As a parent, the thought a child passing from this world is hard enough to come to terms with, let alone the very thought of them arriving in the Afterworld with no one there to meet them or not knowing what to do, where to go or what to expect. Children perceive things very differently to the way adults do. Sometimes what we see as confronting, a child's perception of it may be one of awe and wonder, while things we may observe as fine, a child will shy away from or be afraid of. An adult may love the spirit of Christmas, for example, while a child may find the sight of a real, live Santa Clause terrifying. It is for this reason that when a child passes, they are escorted by a Spirit Guide from the outset, with no stone left unturned to ensure their safety and wellbeing.

Depending on the experiences the child endured during their short life, the need for their United Element to visit the Underworld may be reduced and their time spent there shortened depending on how they passed and why. Or it could depend on their age where they are eliminated from the equation due to the simple fact they wouldn't have a reason to partake in the challenges found there. Their age may also affect the amount of time they spend time in a nursery on arrival at the Great Hall, in order to be closely attended to by the Healers whose job it is to help them adjust to an existence without parents, or their mother at least, and to ensure their life force remains good and strong.

These factors aside, it is my belief that every other aspect of their journey to the Afterworld is the same as that of an adult, except that children may appear to grow up or grow older the longer they stay in the Afterworld (perhaps as a way of reassuring grieving parents of their wellness), whereas adults seem to appear younger, healthier and more vibrant.

PART THREE

Manifestations of Spirit

There's a belief that I would like to explore, one that suggests that many of those once considered Faeries may have actually been spirits of the dearly departed or some other manifestation of the dead, observed walking among the living.

The Banshee, for example, (from the Irish *bean sídhe*, which means 'Woman of the Síde', 'Woman of the Faery Mounds', or simply 'Faery Woman') is a spirit from Irish mythology that comes as a harbinger of death and a messenger from the Otherworld. In times long gone, it was common for the people to bury their chieftains and other significant members of the tribe atop small hills known as barrows. Although they gradually forgot the significance of these hills as generations passed, the hills continued to emit memory of their sacred purposes. The people felt this sacredness and came to view them as passageways to the land of the dead and, similarly, the realm of Faerie.

I once read of a man, whose name and details I can no longer find, who was reported to have been taken by the Faeries and, upon his return, was recorded saying that whenever he stood and stared long enough at the Faeries, they eventually revealed themselves to be neighbours, friends and family members that had died years before. This account got me thinking and, while I know in my heart the Faerie realm exists in its own right, it made sense that the dead could easily have been confused with the Fae, and vice versa, being that they're both of this world but are not, and are spiritual as much as they are physical.

The Faerie realm

Also known as The Fae, The Fay, The Fey, The Subterraneans, The Grey Neighbours, The Good Neighbours, The Fair Folk, The Good Folk, The Wee Folk, The Good People, The Small People, The Old People, The People of Peace, The People of the Hills, The Gentry, The Seelie Court, They, Them, Them Ones, Themselves, Them That's In It, The Littles, The Borrowers, The Others, The Strangers and The Cipenapers, many people tend to describe the Faeries as small magical human-like beings with delicate wings that flutter joyfully from one flower to the next.

I guess it's safe to say that in today's world, most people associate Faeries, in one form or another, with the flowers, trees and plants of the garden, wilderness and parkland.

A lot of books on the subject support that belief, explaining that every plant and flower has its own Faerie that either protects it or resides deep within its essence. So much so that illustrations often depict them dressed in clothing that's either inspired by the colours and design of the flower they're associated with or cloaked in petals, leaves and stamens of the flowers themselves.

As sweet as the thought of flower Faeries are, though, the original Faeries were depicted very differently; either as beings as tall as the average adult human, radiant and lithe with pale complexions and fair hair or as short, dark, wrinkled, earthy dwarf-like creatures the average height of a six-year-old human child. The early Faeries were rarely depicted with wings, as opposed to the more modern-day Faeries that invariably sport butterfly or dragonfly wings. The very small Faeries, if they were seen flying, were more often than not described as riding on enchanted twigs, ragwort stems or on the backs of small birds.

The term Faerie hasn't always been reserved for only the 'Little People': Ghosts, Phantoms, Goblins, Brownies, Elves, Trolls, Selkies, Kelpies, Centaurs, Unicorns and even Dragons were once all labelled collectively as Faeries.

One belief is that Faeries are no different from the elemental spirits of Earth, Air, Fire and Water. To those who practised alchemy, for example, the Faeries were often grouped together in elementally attuned baskets, with Gnomes ruling Earth, Sylphs ruling the Air, Salamanders ruling Fire and Undines ruling the Water. Faeries – particularly those associated with deity and spirits of the land – are often connected to the rivers, lakes, oceans and streams (the water), the mountains, valleys, caves, cliffs, forests and ravines (the earth); to the night sky, the morning sky, to wind, storms, thunder and lightning (the air); or to volcanos, the hearth, the kitchen, sexual activity and the resulting offspring and passion (fire). And while this theory still holds true for many people today, the notion of them being more like 'spirits of the air' has a wider acceptance, hence being so often depicted with delicate insect-like wings.

Described as being as bright and radiant and fairer than the sun itself, there is a race of Faeries known as the Light Elves who exist in a realm located halfway between Heaven and Earth and who are said to be in constant communication with the gods. So much so, people once looked to them as others might look to Angels. Despite this, however, some believe that while not entirely suited to Heaven and not totally deserving of Hell, the Faeries exist midway and are welcomed to remain in neither. The story is that at some point, God decided that the beings in Heaven would be referred to as Angels and those in Hell would be known as Demons... while those in between would be banished to Earth, where they became known as Faeries.

Some people defend their belief in 'evil' Faeries or those that intentionally live to deceive and cause harm. The Hobgoblin is one such example. Once deemed a humble and helpful household Faerie, an ancestral family spirit of the hob or kitchen hearth, the Hobgoblin became the mischievous, malevolent creature it is today after its energy was changed from respectable to wicked by the church. It is still believed by many that all Faeries fear and avoid the sound of church bells – being that they're not 'of God' – but not the Hobgoblin who is said to blatantly flout the church and harass its people in a similar fashion to the Devil.

Others believe that the gods and goddesses of the early religions became the Faeries described in the stories told by the descendants of the original Pagan tribes as a way of honouring their memory and hiding their devotion to the Fae from the Christian church. To this day, many of the gods and goddesses of Celtic tradition hold strong association with the rivers and streams, trees, flowers, mountains, valleys and lakes. The church labelled devotees of these gods and goddesses 'pagan witches' and many, like Joan of Arc, found themselves burned at the stake for their blasphemous beliefs, while the deities they celebrated were relegated to the rank of 'demon'.

In the Highlands the Faeries are called the Sith. In Cornwall they're referred to as Pisgies while the Irish know them as the Sidhe or Sidh (pronounced *shee*), which translates to hill-dweller, a name that's probably a result of their prehistoric practice of burying significant members of their tribes atop small hills known as barrows. Over time the burial mounds became 'tomb-wombs', sacred hills of rebirth offering a chance and opportunity to start over. As such, they became places where wishes could be granted at certain times of the year. Samhain, a festival that marked the end of the harvest season and celebration of the dead, became one such time when the Veil between our world and the realm of Faerie is known to be at its thinnest. Faerie mounds such as these are purportedly ablaze with light during Samhain, lit by thousands of tiny flaming torches and alive with the sound of playful music, dance and laughter.

Although the people forgot the tradition of honouring their chieftains in this way as time went on, the small hills continued to emit memory of their sacred origins. The people, of course, felt this sacredness and so began the belief that the barrows were portholes or doorways to the Otherworld where the gods and goddesses, Nature Spirits and Ancestors were thought to dwell. The Other-world (sometimes linked with or referred to as the Isle of Apples and known also as Avalon in Arthurian legend) can be entered by living mortals by means of a magical Silver Bough (which also offered the living mortal safe passage to leave). Apparently, the Faerie Queen would on occasion offer the sacred branch to deserving living mortals, allowing them to come and go at will.

Folklore has it that the Sidhe have walked among us since the beginning of time. Like the Angels, they probably overlooked the birth of the Earth Mother herself. Said to be shape-changers, the Sidhe can appear small or large, as humans, birds, animals, insects or fish, as wind, rain or snow... even as dead loved ones. Such Creator Spirits are common characters in most ancient origin-of-life stories, including The Dreamtime legends of the Ind-igenous Australians. Although they inhabit the ancient grassy mounds, or barrows – several hundred of which dot the Irish countryside, the homeland of the Sidhe is called Tir-na-nog (also known as the Country of the Young or the Land of Youth) in Irish tradition. Where this place is, no one knows for sure. Some say it's under the ground, while others say it's under the sea. The Sidhe are known to receive gifts of food as well as morsels that are unavailable...

and while anything and everything is generally well received, they never touch salt. In return, they're known to happily cure humans of illness and disease and to help them with their daily tasks, to find wealth and even help relocate lost livestock. Although they were sometimes referred to as the *Tuatha de Danann* (beings that come as close to being described as gods and goddesses as any other in Irish myth and legend), the Sidhe were usually simply referred to as Faeries.

The Djinn

According to Middle Eastern mythology, the Djinn (from the Arabic *Junna*, meaning 'angry' or 'possessed') are said to have existed on Earth eons before the birth of humanity and were described in folklore long before they were ever mentioned in Islamic religious texts. There are several types of Djinn. Among them: the *Ghul* – a shape-shifting, trouble-making spirit (*Ghul* is the origin of the word 'Ghoul' or 'Ghost'); the *Sil* – a Djinn that cannot change shape; the *Ifrit* – an evil spirit, and the *Marid* – considered the most powerful Djinn of all.

While man was once believed to have been born from the clay of the earth, the Djinn are said to be disruptive spirit beings formed of smokeless fire. Like man, the Djinn are bestowed with free will which allows them to go about their business and behave as they please. They can believe whatever they want to believe and associate with whomever they choose.

Like most spirit beings, the Djinn are invisible to humans and, apparently, humans are almost always invisible to the Djinn. However, when they do make themselves visible to humans, they will often appear in human form or as an animal. While Djinn are not ghosts perse, they are considered to be 'spirits'. Now, whether that means they are spirits of the dearly departed or the spirits of land isn't clear, but what most are sure about is that they are spirits nonetheless.

Apart from sharing the gift of free will with humans, there are several factors that link the Djinn with the spirits of the human dead. One is that they're often associated with graveyards and, along with humanity, they're destined to be judged according to their earthly behaviour on the 'Day of Judgment'. While they're known to be troublesome and injurious toward humans on occasion, they're mostly in agreement with the ways of humans and can be very supportive of them, guiding them on a creative level (especially when it comes to the written word). So, based on their deeds while on Earth, the Djinn know that their chances of going to 'Hell' as opposed to 'Heaven' at the end of days are just as likely for them as it is for any human being.

Along with humans too, they also share the chance of rebirth. Pre-Islamic mythology doesn't distinguish between deity and demon, so the Djinn are considered to be deity of inferior rank, due largely to the human-like qualities they possess. Like humans, the Djinn sniff and taste things. They drink, eat, toilet themselves and sleep. When eating, they always use their left hand. They also produce offspring (it's even possible for them to take human lovers and have children to them). Shunning daylight, avoiding salt and steel and detesting the sound of human song, the Djinn are said to live in community groups in isolated mountainous regions, on the surface of deep bodies of water, in dense forested areas or inside the trees themselves, high in the air or deep within the earth.

While I'm best known for my love of animal symbology and my ability to see Spirit Animals since I was a child, could it be that I've had a personal Djinn following me all this time? Could it be that the many etheric animals I see when I look at people are all the one Djinn, showing itself to me in a plethora of different forms, archetypically revealing the personality of the different people I meet over the course of a day? Could it be that I see many different animal forms... but that it is the same Djinn every time, shape-shifting in accordance with the individual energy of the person or people? All I know is that if I do have a Djinn watching over me, it has done nothing but protect me, guide me, inspire me and offer me ways to heal, and for that, I will be forever grateful.

Angels

An Angel is a spiritual creature created
by God without a body, for the service of
Christendom and of the Earth. They
rescue, guard, keep, protect, bring us
messages from God, fight our battles,
and carry out God's desires. –
Martin Luther King

The word Angel comes from the Greek word, *Angelos*, meaning 'messenger'. Angels have long been revered as heralds of God; guiding lights that inspire, heal and fight for justice. Winged human-like beings radiating halos of white light, Angels appear in most major religions, playing important roles in Creation. Revered in Judeo-Christianity, for example, Angels appear in both the Old and New Testaments and are believed to belong to a celestial hierarchy of nine main Orders. According to the New Testament, all Celestial Beings are grouped into seven ranks: Angels, Archangels, Principalities, Powers, Virtues, Dominions and Thrones. The Old Testament adds Cherubim and Seraphim, which, when combined with the other seven ranks, comprise the nine choirs of Angels in latter Christian theology (although the number typically remains fixed at seven). According to the book of Rev-elations, there were seven Angels that stood before God. Who these Angels were remains a mystery because different texts quote different Angels. The Angels most commonly agreed upon, though, became known as Archangels; divine messengers that sustained a line of communication between humanity and God while combating negativity in the form of confusion, fear, grief, greed, anger, frustration, abuse, control and tyranny.

Very few Angels were referred to by their true name in early sacred texts, as doing so was thought to lessen their power. When called upon, Angels are said to guide, heal and inspire, their wisdom rousing clarity and creativity. Seeking Angelic support has been incorporated into spiritual belief since the Middle Ages, with Jesus himself claiming the ability to invoke 12 legions or 72,000 Angels when required.

Spirit Guides

According to Western culture, it is the role of the Angels to implement the will of God and they do this by acting as envoys, Guardians and Guides. Despite being best known for doing God's will, Angels are believed to be non-denominational, so essentially anyone can call upon them, including your Guardian Angel, for guidance, support and protection, no matter who or what you believe in or pray to.

As formerly mentioned, I grew up surrounded by Spirit Animals and honestly thought everyone could see them. It was not until later that I realised they couldn't. As I matured, my ability to see the animals came and went until my mid-twenties when I was forced to notice, listen and honour them as my 'medicine' and a way for me to follow my path and honour my connection to Spirit. Just as there are Spirit Animals with the acumen to assist us in every aspect of our lives, as teachers, Totems and Guides, the animals that physically share our Earth with us are equally imbued with wisdom potent enough to navigate us successfully and abundantly through life. For years I have been visited (on the Astral Plane) by a black jaguar that has crystal-blue eyes and, on occasion, a translucent apple-green tree snake. For the longest time I didn't take much notice of them because it wasn't out of the ordinary for me to see animals in or around my home; Spirit Animals that no one else could see. And then it struck me – jaguars don't normally have blue eyes. So, you can imagine my surprise when I finally asked it one day: 'Who are you?' only to hear his straightforward reply: 'Michael'. And not to be outdone, the surprise continued when the tree snake introduced himself curtly as 'Raphael'.

In truth, it doesn't matter whether you choose to seek guidance from the Angels, Spirit Animals, your Ancestors, the Faeries, the Djinn or the Sidhe (who can appear in any form they choose), they can all be grouped under the single banner of Spirit Guide. According to most spiritualists, Spirit Guides are beings that choose to remain disembodied spirits in order to take on the role of guide or protector to living people. Stereotypical Spirit Guides often include Native American chiefs, Buddhist monks, Ancient Egyptian deity, or any number of Ascended Masters, saints and other enlightened people from history, but in most cases, they are described as beings of pure energy, 'light beings' or beings of higher vibration than anyone of human descent.

Others believe that when a person has incarnated many times and has learned all the lessons they can learn, they may be offered the chance to become a Spirit Guide to someone still living. There are also others who still denounce the whole notion of Spirit Guides, or spirits who exist to do nothing but assist the living, as being degrading to both the living and the dead.

Demons

While it has been said that a Demon in one religion may be considered deity in another, the belief in Demons (a term derived from the Greek *Daimon*) is as old as religion itself. In its purest form, the word Demon once described any otherworldly being that offered clarity, insight, direction and purpose.

Over time, the description has changed to mean and include any being that refused to be controlled or retitled by the church and that have, as a result, been exiled from Heaven and branded as 'Fallen Angels'. Once describing an unpredictable force that may be summoned and repressed to some degree, the word now refers to a being or source of pure evil, or to personifications of Devil himself; a non-physical spirit of a malevolent and volatile nature or a sinister energy capable of possessing the mind, body and spirit of an animal or human. Like a parasitic tick riding, feeding, crippling and eventually killing a hapless dog, Demons are today blamed as the transmitters of disease responsible for the causation of countless forms of physical, mental, emotional and spiritual debilitation.

Daemons

Have you read the book *The Northern Lights* (from Philip Pullman's trilogy, 'His Dark Materials' first published in 1995 by Scholastic) or seen the 2007 movie, *The Golden Compass*? Both versions tell the story of a little girl named Lyra who lives in a world not that dissimilar to ours, except that in her world all the people are accompanied everywhere they go by an animal; an animal that is essentially an extension of their being, or more to the point – a physical externalised representation of their soul. In Lyra's world, these animals are easily seen. They're physical in form, mirroring the character, beliefs and even the jobs of the people they accompany. In our world, too, we are accompanied by similar animals but, very few among us can see them.

Patrick Harpur, author of *The Philosophers' Secret Fire;*

A History of the Imagination (most recently published by Blue Angel Publishing, Australia), describes Angels and similar beings as falling into a category he calls Daemons or Daimons. Daemons, he explains, are both tangible and intangible, material and immaterial – meaning you can see them but you can't touch them – are both feminine and masculine in nature and are both 'here' but not 'from here'. Faeries, land spirits, elemental spirits and even aliens also known as ETs or 'little green men' can all be described as Daemons, says Harpur, because they're all illustrated as being 'as much physical as spiritual'. He describes Daemons, in their truest form, as being 'elusive, contradictory [and], shape-shifting'. He writes:

> By the second century AD... virtually everyone, pagan, Jewish, Christian or Gnostic... believed in the existence of these beings and in their function as mediators, whether he called them Daemons or Angels or aions or simple "spirits". The Romans, for example, conceived of an almost infinite number of divine beings.

He then quotes Socrates:

> ...we have no contact with the gods or God except through the Daemons who "interpret and convey the wishes of men to the gods and the will of gods to men..." Only through the gods is there conversation between men and gods, whether in the waking state or during sleep.

Harpur then concludes that: 'Anyone who is an expert in such converse is a "daemonic man"' and decided that Swiss psychologist C.G. Jung was a perfect and obvious example of this. Apparently, Jung regularly dreamed of a Daemon: a winged man with horns who visited him during his waking hours as well as in his sleep. He appeared quite real and physical in nature at times and would follow Jung as he walked through his garden. Jung said of the visits:

> He brought me the crucial insight that there are things in the psyche which I do not produce, but which have a life of their own, like animals in the forest or people in a room. It was he who taught me psychic objectivity, the reality of the psyche.

In his book, Harpur also introduces us to The Reverend Robert Kirk who in 1961 published the first study of Faeries: *The Secret Commonwealth of Elves, Fauns and Fairies*. Kirk described Daemons in his work as being 'of a middle nature betwixt man and Angell'. 'All pagans once recognised a multitude of Daemons which mediated between them and their many gods', he wrote, and then continued to explain that the exile of Daemons began with the birth of Christianity. You see, for those of the Christian faith, the only tolerable mediator between man and God was Jesus Christ. So, over time the word Daemon, which by its original definition explains a heavenly being that offers clarity, insight, direction and purpose, was systematically bastardised and refashioned to mean Demon and referred instead to something that refused to be tamed, renamed or banished; beings that have come to be feared as Fallen Angels and Devils.

Ghosts

Ghosts or spirits are said to be the souls or spirits of people or animals that have died, but that can still be seen or sensed by the living as an invisible presence, a transparent, smoke-like form or a genuine, almost corporal apparition. Based on the observation that ghosts appear to be fashioned from a cloudy, wispy, almost air-like substance, it was once believed that they were the embodiment of the person that lives within the person, also known as the person's spirit or the person's breath which, in frosty weather, can be seen exiting the mouth as a kind of ethereal mist.

Communication with the Other Side by George 1st Baron Lyttelton and published in England in 1760, is the earliest known book that describes the living attempting to contact or communicate with the dead via séance and mediumship. While their existence is impossible to prove or fabricate, science is of the consensus that ghosts, as the disembodied spirits of the dead, do not exist. Usually described as solitary, humanoid spectres, ghosts are believed to haunt places, people or things they were familiar with or most fond of in life. Alternatively, they were also once believed to be deceased people seeking retribution, or the trapped spirits of bad people who were not permitted to enter Heaven.

Despite the Bible referencing the Spirit of God as the Holy Ghost, superstition has it that the sighting of a ghost is a bad omen or even a warning of death, particularly if the sighting appears to be that of your own ghostly double, 'doppelgänger' or 'fetch'.

The reason I didn't include ghosts in the chapter titled the Soul, the Spirit and the United Element is because I personally don't believe in ghosts. I mean, I do... but not the notion of a ghost being the same thing as a deceased person's spirit or disembodied soul. In my opinion, the difference lies in the way a person's spirit interacts with the living as opposed to the way a ghost doesn't.

Ghost stories often tell of haunted houses or spooky places where an apparition is said to appear night after night, religiously doing the same thing such as standing at the top of a stair case, walking up a lane or hallway, or standing in front of a widow. And reports of spirits of those we love often tell of spontaneous or unexpected sightings or visitations, usually centred on crucial life events, rites of passage, significant anniversaries or special events. Ghosts appear to be trapped in a kind of wraithlike 'Groundhog Day', repeating the same action or deed again and again, while a spirit has free will to do what it wants, when it wants, how it wants.

I believe a ghost is effectively an etheric imprint of sorts that's captured for eternity in the energetic make-up of a place or space; the shadow, memory or residual electromagnetic trace of a person who, for whatever reason, repeated the same habitual motion before their death, following the same process or was seen doing the same thing day in, day out, without a break. Examples may include going to the toilet while alive, every night at the same time and being heard walking up the hall by family and friends, or checking the mailbox at the same time every day for a letter that never came before offering salutations to expectant neighbours, or standing at a window daily, waiting for a long-gone family member to return home, and waving at regular passers-by who may have walked their dog every evening or partook in their exercise regime at the same time each morning. The point is, those that witnessed or heard these processes on an unfailing daily basis would have been unconsciously waiting to for it to happen. They would have been expecting, like clockwork, to hear those footsteps, to offer that wave or to bid that familiar 'Good morning'. It's as if the mind of the onlooker becomes almost programmed to see or hear the person, and so even after their death – particularly if they are unaware of the other's passing – not only will that programming endure, it will continue to provide reward, with the 'ghost' of the person still being waved at, smiled at or heard going to the bathroom at the same time each night.

As a kid, I remember being confused as to why my step-grandmother would sit at her bedroom window every day, all day, crocheting. I remember asking why she lifted the curtain before peering out every time someone stopped at the letterbox or paused as they walked past the gate. I thought she was just an old sticky-beak, who enjoyed knowing everything everyone in the neighbourhood was doing. But the truth of the matter was that she sat in that chair every day like a sentry keeping watch, hoping someday to see the son she had lost during the war, whose body was never recovered, return home. My grandmother yearned so deeply to see him walking up the driveway toward the front door that she must have rehearsed the scene in her mind thousands of times, despite having received the dreaded black-edged letter the authorities sent informing her the ship had been struck by a torpedo and sunk. Over time, many of the people who passed by the house grew so accustomed to her peering out at them, they would smile and offer a wave. Even after her death, they would still wave when they saw her lift the curtain.

Haunted houses

Our house wasn't haunted after my step-grandmother died, but people continued to see her. Her spirit wasn't in or haunting our house, but rather the ghost or memory of her yearning was. It was as if the house was holding memory of her grief, re-enacting her heartfelt need to see her son one more time. Like the original screensavers on the older computer monitors that were required to prevent phosphor burn-in, my grandmother's ghost was like the phosphor burn-in, resulting in the last action before her death becoming vibrationally imprinted on the energetic make-up of that particular part of the house because the screensaver didn't kick in. I believe that whenever someone sits quietly in that front room they may be surprised to feel my grandmother's presence or if, for whatever reason, someone stops at the gate and looks toward the front window, they may see her looking back at them from behind the glass. But if they do, I believe it won't be because the house is haunted. Instead, it will be because they've unwittingly tapped into my grandmother's emotional pain and her memories that will be forever be energetically stored in the foundations and earth on which the house stands.

Indigenous Australian people traditionally viewed Creation as based on a sacred 'power of seed' which was deposited deep in the Earth Mother at the beginning of her Dreaming. With the power of this seed, every worldly event or life progression that occurred left behind a residue of its energy within Earth – a record or memory of its happening or existence. This belief was relevant to the principal that plants leave an image of themselves within the earth as seeds. The very make-up of the landscape; every mountain, rock, river, and tree and the vibrational memory of their forming, endorsed the proceedings that birthed that place within Creation. Everything of the natural world was read as a symbolic diary, acted out in the beginning by Spirit Beings – the Ancestors – that formed the world. As with the tiny seed, the fertility of a place was weighed against the memory of its origin. This was called The Dreaming, which represented the sacred core of Earth Mother. Similarly, for me, the vibrational memory of my step-grandmother's life (and that of every person who ever lived and died on the planet) was embodied in the 'power of seed' that, at the exact moment of her death, was deposited in the earth where her bedroom was built. It wasn't deposited into the floorboards of the house or buried in the carpet that lay under her rocking chair, but rather placed deep within the soil under the foundations of the home, directly under the spot where she sat every day, silently dealing with the pain of her ever-breaking heart.

No matter what is true and what is not, I find it interesting to note that the word ghost is pronounced in the north of England as guest.

Spirit Animals

There are other manifestations of spirits that many of us may have seen or experienced, without realising their significance or greater purpose. These manifestations are so familiar we may notice them but fail to associate them with the Afterworld and that's because as animals, we associate them with the living rather than the dead.

Known collectively as psychopomps, these animals can include toads and rats, mainly because of their reputation as being creatures of the night that inhabit mysterious, dark and gloomy places such as swamps, marshes, gutters and drains or areas thought to be haunted, 'spooky' or best avoided by the living.

Due to their underground existence, moles were also once thought to be messengers of the Underworld and emissaries of death itself. Other creatures include red foxes and hares; animals that despite sharing a hunter/prey relationship, are often seen short distances apart when both parents are in spirit, having either died together or a short time apart, or when an anniversary of one or the other's passing is looming. The fox usually refers to the male or masculine energy, the father or father figure, while the hare typically symbolises the female or feminine energy, the mother or mother figure, being that the hare is 'ruled' by the moon, while the moon's 28-day rotation mirrors the sacred feminine cycle of all women.

Cloaked entirely in black, both the raven and the crow are also common Soul Guides recognised as envoys of the sacred Void and messengers of the spirits that exist there, particularly the spirits of the elder women that listen for and respond to prayers for healing, change and awakening. Because their jet-black feathers resemble the robes of both executioners and judges, and due to their habit of congregating around rubbish dumps, funerary sites and gloomy places, the spirits of the raven and crow can also herald justice, closure, endings and even death itself. Looking at things from a polar-opposite perspective is a bird considered so gentle, pure and virtuous because of their snow-coloured plumage, the white dove could be the ultimate Soul Guide for children or those of an innocent heart.

White and albino animals have been revered in most cultures for centuries; venerated as omens of good fortune, fertility, plentiful rain, bountiful harvest or believed to be imbued with supernatural or magical powers. In medieval Europe, for example, it was believed that white mice personified the souls of departed children, while in Thailand, it is believed that white elephants may contain the souls of people who have crossed over to the Afterworld. White animals appear regularly in Welsh and Celtic mythology too, as creatures of Underworld, often charged with extraordinary strength, speed, shape and size and sporting glowing red ears, eyes and snouts, that when seen in the physical world, were more often than not pursued by brave warriors and noblemen. To hunt a white stag, for example, either metaphorically or physically, was once considered symbolic of the journey we will all eventually take into the Underworld; a journey that will see us stalk our limitations and overcome our inherent obstacles and fears.

Associated with the night, the moon and in-between places, the spirits of both cats and owls are linked by myth and legend as escorts of spirits and guardians of the entrances to the Otherworlds. Energetically one and the same (hence why the Owl and the Pussycat could marry, bear children and sail away together in their pea-green boat), both are said to offer safe passage to the souls of the departed as they embark on their journey to the Afterworld. In similar fashion, bats and owls share a relationship according to some Indigenous Australian nations or language groups, with the bat, particularly the snow-white ghost bat, representing the masculine spirit of brothers, sons, uncles, fathers and grandfathers, nephews and grandsons, and the owl, a feminine spirit, symbolising the spirit of daughters, aunts, mothers and grandmothers, nephews and granddaughters. Incidentally, the spirit of the owl is also (by some nations or language groups) seen as a protector of children, while barn owls are also known as 'ghost owls' and horned owls are said to only roost in haunted buildings.

Other creatures synonymous with the journey to the Afterworld are bees, butterflies, dragonflies and, to a lesser degree, moths. Moths are often seen congregating around street lamps, ceiling lights and outdoor spotlights, a happening that I associate with the soul's quest to reconnect and return to the Creator, the Source or the Light. Bees were once revered as bridges between the natural world and the Underworld. Images of bees once adorned the walls of tombs, and it was believed that bees embodied the souls of priestesses who had lived their lives dedicated to the goddess Aphrodite. Butterflies and dragonflies, however, are said to mirror the soul's journey in that they start life as Earthbound organisms (or in the case of the dragonfly, a water nymph) before dying to their former selves to re-emerge as seemingly completely different life forms; almost angelic or faerie-like winged beings. As the caterpillar builds its chrysalis, for example, it entombs itself, shutting itself off from the world of the living, during which time it surrenders all trace of its former self, before eventually breaking free to emerge as a transformed soul; a metamorphous journey that's very similar to the death of the body and the emergence of the spirit that can't help but rise to the heavens like a butterfly taking flight for the first time.

Being that they're all carrion eaters, creatures that inherently know it's their job to clean up the remains of animals that have been killed or dies of natural causes – opossums, vultures, hyenas, Tasmanian devils, hawks, eagles and coyotes are by the pure nature of their roles, also symbolically charged with the responsibility of ushering the spirits of the dead to the Afterworld. In a similar fashion but for different reasons, jackals have long been associated with the dead, as a Guardian of the Underworld because they were regularly seen haunting areas where tombs had been recently built. The jackal is also the 'animal-form' of Anubis, the Egyptian jackal-headed god of the Underworld, embalming and mummification who was responsible for the handling of the balances that weighed the hearts of the departed against the Feather of Maat; the Mother of Truth.

Perhaps named after the same god is *Papio Anubis* the baboon, who also holds strong association with the Afterworld. According to Ancient Egyptian lore, the god Thoth took the form of a baboon when listening to appeals in the Judgment Hall of Osirus in the land of the dead, as one of the Four Sacred Apes that sat in council beside the Lake of Fire. Overlooked by the Throne of Osirus, the baboon listened to all petitions put forward by the souls and determined who was worthy to pass into the Other Worlds.

As a land-dwelling animal and an aquatic one that holds its own links to the Ancient Egyptian notion of the

Afterworld, the crocodile can also be seen as the guardian of the subtle door that offers passage from the physical world to the Underworld; the embodiment of both life and death in their purest forms.

Likewise, it was not uncommon in early stories for the hero of a story to be swallowed by a whale, with their journey into the creature's belly being symbolic of their descent into the Underworld and the death of their familiar self, with their eventual re-emergence representing their ultimate rebirth. While, and according to Roman mythology, the peacock was sacred to the Mother goddess Juno, who was said to weigh the peacock's tail feathers against the hearts of men to determine their integrity and their worthiness to travel to the Underworld.

Also associated with the Underworld is the black pig or black sow, a harbinger of unequivocal endings that must be endured before the soul can experience regeneration of any kind. Indicative of the goddess in her crone phase and the chapter of life that constitutes wisdom and maturity that comes with old age, the black sow embodies the mystical journey that culminates in the divine death of the familiar self, the ending of cycles or the completion of one phase so that another may commence, such the transition or rite of passage that sees a maiden become a mother or a mother become a crone, while her mate, the boar, was said to offer those wandering through the Underworld the knowledge and transformational power to face and slay their inner demons with the determination befitting a true warrior. In keeping with the pig theme, piglets can be considered buds of new growth, or the beginning of a new cycle, an unexpected pregnancy or issues centred on children. As such, in similar fashion to the sparrow, the piglet can symbolise the spirit of children, or be viewed as a protector of the spirit of children, while bears are often the form the spirit of a father or father figure (or their Soul Guide) may take, while the Soul Guide or spirit of a mother or mother figure may adopt the likeness of a cow.

Signs, Omens
and
Confirmations

Sometimes it's impossible to know for sure if our loved ones in spirit are with us or not, and whether they are aware of what's happening in our lives or if they're watching over us and our family. In the hope that it offers some comfort, I like to believe that when you find yourself thinking of someone (be they alive or dead), then there's a big chance they're thinking of you too. But, if you're the sort of person that needs physical proof, there are a few things you can watch out for that could be taken as signs or subtle forms of confirmation that you're not alone.

The Fox Sisters: Mothers of mediumship and spirituality

The Fox Sisters: Leah (1831–1890), Margaret (or Maggie, 1833–1893) and Kate (or Catherine, 1837–1892) Fox, were three sisters from New York who played a significant hand in the birth and rise of the Spiritualist movement. When they were children, the two younger sisters – Kate (then aged 12) and Margaret (aged 15) lived with their parents in Hydesville, New York, a hamlet that no longer exists.

The girl's house had earned itself the reputation of being haunted, but it wasn't until March 1848 that the family were frightened by unexplained knocking sounds that sounded like someone was moving furniture about. The younger sisters told Kate that through 'rappings' they were able to communicate with the spirits of the dead. So persuaded was Kate that she willingly took up the mantle of manager and oversaw their career as professional mediums until Margaret and Kate confessed to making the whole thing up and publicly admitted that the rappings were a hoax.

On retiring for the night, the sisters purported that they would tie an apple to a string and by pulling on the string, would cause the apple to rise and fall onto the floor of their room creating a bumping sound. Their mother, who was confused by the sound, never once suspected her daughters. And even when Kate challenged whatever or whoever was making the noises to repeat the snaps of her fingers and to rap out her age, their mother never doubted their innocence.

Identifying the source of the rappings to be a spirit they dubbed 'Mr Splitfoot' – a nickname for the Devil – the girls soon attracted the attention of their neighbours who discovered the rappings could answer simple questions by means of a 'one for a yes, two for a no' response, or represent the letters of the alphabet. The mystery deepened further when the girls claimed Mr Splitfoot was in fact the spirit of a man called Charles B. Rosna, a murdered pedlar whose body was buried in their cellar. According to reports penned by Arthur Conan Doyle, the neighbours dug up the cellar and found a few bones, but it wasn't until 1904 when a skeleton was found entombed in the cellar wall that the girls' story was taken seriously, even though no person by the name of Charles B. Rosna was ever reported missing. A tin box said to have been owned by the supposed peddler was also found in the cellar and now rests in the Lily Dale Museum, New York; a camp and meeting place founded in 1879 where spiritualists and freethinkers could gather to further the science, philosophy and religion of Spiritualism.

Despite Margaret's desperate attempts to recant her confession a year later, the sisters' reputation had been ruined beyond repair and less than five years later, after Margaret and Kate's decline into a wretched state of poverty, all three sisters were dead.

Notwithstanding their fall from grace, the Fox Sisters had inadvertently given rise to the Spiritualism movement, which continued to grow in force and popularity after their death. Whether the Fox Sisters were frauds or not, no one can deny the wave of fascination and fame they earned during their short career as mediums.

Demonstrating their supernatural rappings in Rochester on 14 November 1849, the sisters were the first to open a channel of communication between our world and that of the dead in front of a large paying public audience – an event that saw the sisters become very famous, while simultaneously triggering a long and healthy history of public shows that launched the careers of countless psychic mediums inside and outside the United States. While their early seances were quite simple, with audience members seeking advice on love and financial investments, the greater, spiritual significance of communing with the dead soon took priority. And the rest, as they say, is history.

Confirmations

Some people light candles in memory to acknowledge the spirit of the dead living on and continuing to burn brightly. According to ancient pagan practice, light is pure, banishes the dark, nurtures life and illuminates the world. Symbolically, the wax of the candle is said to represent the body, the wick is the soul and, the flame is the spirit or life force of the person who's passed. Keeping all this in mind, the candle flame has long been a favourite indicator of whether we are alone or not, being that when the flame burns tall and still, there's no presence but when it flickers and dances about, without environmental disturbance such as a breeze, then perhaps there is. Likewise, when the globes in electric ceiling lights or lamps start to inexplicably flicker, especially when the dead come up in conversation, the consensus among spiritualists is that they are making their presence known.

Following a similar theme, a friend of mine knew when her father was with her because he would ring the doorbell. Naturally, she would always check to see if anyone was physically at the door before assuming it was her dad, but on those occasions when there was no one there, she found peace in the knowing her dad was paying her a visit from the Spirit World.

And finally, another friend knows when a spirit is supporting her healing work because her CD player will mysteriously change tracks (often to a song that mirrors what the client is needing healing for), or her TV will turn itself on. On a similar note (no pun intended), hearing a loved one's favourite song randomly play on the radio, or a song that was played at their funeral, especially when they're in your thoughts or it's around the time of their birthday or some other significant anniversary or date, is about as close to a guarantee as I can give that your loved one is watching over you.

Signs

Repeatedly finding coins, also known as 'pennies from Heaven', in usual places may become a recognisable sign that a loved one is close, especially if it's the same denomination each time. The same thing can be said for seeing falling stars when you're thinking of a loved one, as well as randomly seeing familiar shapes formed by clouds on significant days or finding feathers in strange or unlikely places. I believe that an arbitrary feather found in a weird location – like on a bus, in the bathroom vanity or in your laptop case – is a sure sign that a spirit is close. A friend of mine was surprised once when she opened her front door to find about 20 white feathers standing upright, their quills pushed firmly into her doormat. After checking with her family and neighbours, it soon became evident that they'd had nothing to do with their peculiar place-ment, and she was left to wonder if a recently departed family member had done it as a way of letting her know they were okay.

Another sign that's worth watching for are significant numbers, or the total sum of significant numbers, such as birthdates, car registration numbers, house numbers, phone prefixes, and so on. The repetitive yet unforeseen appearance of these numbers, in whatever order or for-mat, can be considered an indicator of your loved one's spirit's presence, just as hearing, seeing or having brought to your attention the name or nickname of your loved one (such as when a baby is born, and their name is announced, or a neighbour or friend mentions a niece or nephew or friend's name, etc).

And lastly, one more indicator is the smell of perfume, aftershave, cigarettes, cigars, alcohol, horse manure (or the smell of stables), engine oil or petrol or essential oils, incenses or herbs such as patchouli, lavender, rosemary, frankincense and myrrh; all these things can inherently remind you of a loved one in spirit, and when that happens, take note because if the brain connects the power of smell to a distinct memory, there's always a relevant reason – and purpose – for that ass-ociation to be made. The thing to remember is that signs such as these need to be taken seriously, no matter how trivial they may feel at the time because the Great Spirit never makes mistakes.

Although there are many people who claim to have been born with the ability to see Spirit, equally as many believe they were not. Cats are said to have the sight, so if you have a close relationship with your cat, you could learn to watch his or her movements and gauge the possibility of spirit activity by their actions and reactions. In a similar manner to how a vision-impaired person gains 'sight' by way of their guide dog, your cat will offer you the sight by proxy. When you spy your cat staring intently at something, for example, and when you follow his or her gaze and there's (apparently) nothing to see, you can be sure it's a spirit that has caught their eye. So, sit still, focus your mind and become one with your cat – and you may be lucky enough to catch a glimpse into the Realm of Spirit through their eyes. There are other certain animals that are traditionally associated with the Spirit World that, despite not being equipped to help you 'see' the spirit of those that have passed away, may appear symbolically to inform you that your loved ones are doing okay, or that they're with you or watching over you.

Dreams

While not a typical place to commune with the dead, it is not uncommon for people to wake from a dream and to feel instinctively that their loved ones have paid them a visit. Some dreams are so vivid that the sleeper may wake with clear memory of being told certain things by their loved ones, warned of upcoming events or reassured that all will be well during times of hardship or worry. And when we are open to the idea of these sorts of experiences being more than just a dream, but rather a 'between the worlds' meeting, then they can become something of a regular occurrence, or at least until the spirit(s) decides or explains otherwise.

I have a reoccurring dream, or rather I have separate dreams in a reoccurring setting, where I visit my friends in a secluded valley that has a wheel house that sits on the edge of a fast-flowing stream. When I realise I am in the valley, I check to see if the wheel is turning and out of the wheel house they emerge. The valley is fully enveloped in birch trees, their branches blocking out the sun and any view of the sky, while the ground is littered with their fallen leaves. My friends told me the first time I met them in the valley that, when the day comes, and the wheel isn't turning, that that would be the last time I saw them. But, until that day arrives, I look forward to the dreams and my visits during which they tell me things, like where I am heading in life and what I need to do when I get there.

Psychopomps

As mentioned earlier, beings known as psychopomps – a Greek word that translates to the 'guide of souls' – can take the form of animals and whose role it is to escort the spirits of our loved ones to the Afterworld. Appearing regularly in funerary art in cultures the world over, psychopomps are often depicted as anthropomorphic creatures. The belief is that when they manifest as birds, they will often be seen congregating in huge flocks on or around the house or building of a person who's about to die. It's for this reason that many people associate winged beings as being symbolically more 'spiritual' than those that aren't. For example, flying horses, Faeries, winged deity and Angels are all considered to be closer to God simply because they have wings and the ability to fly, just as eagles are often associated with the Creator because they fly the highest and closest to the sun than any other bird.

When my mother-in-law passed away after a long battle with cancer, I was determined to identify the animal that was to become my symbol for her spirit so that when I saw it, I'd know without a doubt it was her. Well, it didn't take long for the blue wren to step forward and to identify itself as her Spirit Animal. Wrens are seen all around the world as symbols of intelligence, strength of mind, endurance, ambition and bravery. A well-known story tells of a competition between some birds to see who could fly closest to the sun. They all knew that the only one truly capable of the task was the eagle, who nobly stood back awaiting his turn while one by one they fell back to Earth, exhausted, burned or dehydrated. The eagle soared until it was evident he had won the competition. He was then surprised to hear a tiny voice say, 'What about me?' A wren was above him, frantically flapping his wings, sweat pouring down his cheeks, his feathers fraying from the heat. Upon landing, the eagle begged the wren to reveal his secret about how he had flown so high. No one had noticed the little bird hiding among the eagle's feathers, trusting that the eagle would not discover him and eat him to hide his defeat. But the eagle recognised the wren's bravery and awarded him the title of 'bravest and most ambitious bird'.

In my first book *Animal Dreaming*, I explain that the wisdom of wren symbolically heralds brand-new challenges and charges us with an unwavering faith in our ability to achieve any goal. This is also true of my mother-in-law who, in life, would have encouraged us to strive for ever-higher goals, to believe in ourselves and to never give up. A symbol of illumination, intuition and the intellect, wren embodies the ability 'to know'. It offers clarity potent enough to dispel confusion and despair forever, allowing us to feel brave and ambitious, no matter how small we believe ourselves to be. And now that she's passed away, whenever my wife and I feel my mother-in-law's presence, we can feel her encouraging us to push forward by offering clarity, wisdom and inner knowledge. As a symbol of illumination and intuition, the fact that the wren stepped forward as my mother-in-law's Spirit Animal makes so much sense because, all those years ago she was one of the influencing factors that put me on my path as a psychic and mystic. How beautiful is that? And what wonderful confirmation.

Those Left Behind

There are two things that cannot be avoided: death and taxes. As cold as that may sound, this famous saying is nothing short of the truth. Everyone and everything dies. Everyone and everything has an expiry date. And what's even worse is that the time and place of our death has long said to be preordained. While we aren't meant to know when our time is up, there's nothing to say we didn't agree to the wheels being set in motion long before we incarnated into this world. And even if we inadvertently do something to delay the inevitable, death will still find us. Say, for example, we are meant to die by train on a Monday on our way to the office, but for some inexplicable reason we decide to take the car, which is our right because according to Universal Law, we are all born with the power of free will. And we make it to work in one piece... but there's nothing to say that the train accident won't still happen resulting in many people dying a tragic death. Have we been spared? Yes, but only temporarily. There's a big chance, for example, that the following Monday we may indeed be killed by a train, but only after we are 'accidently' pushed from the platform onto the tracks by an unsuspecting passenger hurrying to get a ticket or when we try to beat the train by rushing through before the boom gates have had a chance to close and our car is hit side-on as it speeds through the intersection.

To have the power to avoid death would result in great unbalance. It would see many things unfold in ways never intended to happen. The entire Universe would need to reshuffle to make our continued existence possible, with many things once destined to happen suddenly unable to take place, and other things that were never meant to be being forced to come to fruition. While no one may notice, the truth of the matter is that if we could avoid death then chaos – albeit potentially undetectable to the everyday soul – would be the order of the day.

We often hear people say of their loved ones who may have just died, 'they went before their time', or 'they died too young'. I remember saying this very the same thing when my friends were killed in the car accident, but they actually didn't. They went at exactly the right time because it was *their* time, as difficult as that was to com-prehend. It was the wrong time for me. It was the right time for their family. And nothing I or anyone else could have done would have altered that truth. It was their fate, their destiny.

Like many people, I had always felt I was intuitive or that I had some degree of sixth sense. Having grown up in a neglectful and abusive household, I had to trust my instincts when it came to making decisions and reacting to stimuli, so I was adept at listening to my gut and following the signs and messages offered by Nature. But I hadn't at that point in my life invested too much faith in my ability to contact and commune with the Spirit World. So, when my friends died, I remember seeking the advice of a psychic medium. I needed to know that they had arrived in the Afterworld safely.

The main difference between a medium and a psychic is that a medium is someone who effectively acts as a mediator between our world and the Spirit World, while a psychic is an individual who is sensitive enough to read another's psyche. And obviously, a psychic medium is a person that's gifted in both areas. The trouble with deciding to visit a medium is being able to trust that the medium you've chosen is both authentic and ethical and it's wise to do some investigation first. Speak to their clients and ask them for testimonials. Google them and see if anyone has written any reviews. Research their level of experience: if they've read for anyone notable and who they may have trained under. Also take the time to see if they have an established presence on social media and, if they do, 'troll' their pages looking for comments, both good and bad. Only when you are totally convinced of the psychic's or medium's credibility should you book in. Sadly, as I had never visited a psychic or medium before, this was a lesson I had to learn the hard way because the medium I went to see was anything but ethical. While the reading she gave was amazing, there were a few things she said that left me wondering what on Earth she was talking about. Overall, though, the reading was great. She described a lot of the things that had happened in detail and was able to get quite specific with some of the more general information she relayed. I went away feeling quite convinced that my friends had indeed made it safely to the Afterworld.

However, several months later, while chatting to my wife's aunt about the reading, she innocently told me she had visited the same medium herself a week or so before my appointment and had told the medium of my pending visit. She went on to tell me she had, at the medium's prompting, revealed much of the information the medium had relayed back to me during my reading. I was gutted, and my wife's aunt was naturally upset. Interestingly, two or three years later I learned that the medium had died of throat cancer.

Be it a psychic or a medium, a tarot card reader, palm reader, a fortune teller or through the power of prayer, most people will seek out the services of a learned person or a sacred place known for its connection to Spirit World it in a bid to contact their dead loved ones. Some will start attending a spiritualist church because as part of their service they usually offer 'platform presentations' where a medium will stand up and bring through messages from loved ones in spirit. Others may seek out a channeller: someone who willingly allows Spirit to enter and temporarily take over their body and use it as a vessel to communicate directly with the living. While others may decide to attend a séance: a meeting at which a group of people will attempt to communicate with the dead by means of an experienced medium. No matter what avenue we choose to take or which services we decide to employ, the motivation is always the same – the need for proof of survival; evidence that the Afterworld exists and that the soul and spirit live on after death. For many, attaining proof of survival is nothing short of a miracle, which often inspires a healing, cathartic quest for spiritual awakening and enlightenment of their own, during which they may seek to develop their own intuition and mediumship skills.

If this is you, it is important to consider that by losing someone close to you, you have honoured a pact made in another lifetime, and that by deciding to explore what happens when we die, you have – without realising it – reached a higher level of understanding. By exploring life after life, you may have begun to question your own mortality and your place in the greater scheme of things. Perhaps you've decided that you want to be remembered long after you have gone and that you want to leave a legacy if not for your own children, but for humanity. Perhaps you've begun to realise that your earthly pursuits have a greater meaning, and that what you do here on Earth goes beyond the physical realms of our world. That what you have endured and the things you have achieved have sent ripples out into the Universe that will continue to be felt for millennia by not just your children and/or theirs, but by all the children ever to be conceived and born.

There Are No Endings, Only Beginnings...

If you have read this far, then it's a fair bet you've not only made the decision to continue living your life to the full in a physical, emotional and spiritual sense, but that you want to know more.

So, consider this: yes, you have experienced death; yes, you are probably still left with questions that remain unanswered; and yes, you've probably begun to question your own mortality; but rest assured, this is not the end of your journey. In fact, it's just the beginning as you explore the greater complexities of life by continuing to investigate the mysteries of death that have plagued humanity since its inception. Perhaps you could join a society that explores the divine and the untraceable journey of the soul. Perhaps you could delve into the unknown to decide for yourself the fate of the soul after a person dies.

While you yourself may not have died to your physical self yet, you can rest assured that you have indeed travelled full circle in knowing that after your own death, your quest for meaning and truth will continue with your potential rebirth and the reliving experience.

About the Author

Scott Alexander King is an author, teacher, practitioner of Earth Medicine, and a Zoomancer – an individual that examines the habits and appearance of animals to help explain or reveal the future path of human beings. As far as he knows, he's the only Zoomancer in Australia and he calls his path ANIMAL DREAMING. Scott lives in the picturesque Northern Rivers district of far north New South Wales (Australia) with his wife, three children and a menagerie of animals.

www.animaldreaming.com

Scott endorses internationally renowned psychic medium Lisa Williams as his spiritual counsel of choice. If you'd like to investigate Lisa's work, visit her official website www.lisawilliams.com

Other titles by Scott Alexander King

Books

Afterworld

Animal Dreaming

Earth Mother Dreaming

Indigo Children and Cheeky Monkeys

World Animal Dreaming

Oracle Cards and Tarot

Animal Dreaming Oracle Cards

Bohemian Animal Tarot

Creature Teacher Cards

Nature's Wisdom Message Cards

Oracle of the Innocent Heart

World Animal Dreaming Oracle Cards

Meditation CDs

Celebrating Australia's WHEEL OF LIFE

Healing with the Animals

Meet your Power Animal